# Understanding The Creation

## In the Beginning...



MENASHE HAR-EL

cartaJerusalem

First published in 2018 by
**CARTA Jerusalem**

Partially excerpted from
*Landscape Nature and Man in the Bible*
Carta Jerusalem 2003


11 Rivka Street, P.O.B. 2500,
Jerusalem 9102401, Israel
E-mail: carta@carta.co.il
www.carta-jerusalem.com

Quotations from the Hebrew Bible follow the King James Version unless otherwise indicated.

Great care has been taken to establish sources of illustrations. If inadvertently we omitted to do so, due credit will be given in the next edition.



ISBN: 978-965-220-895-8

Printed in Israel

# CONTENTS

*"They go up by the mountains; they go down by the valleys..."* (Psalms 104:8) (photo Samuel Magal).

# INTRODUCTION

The Land of Israel, which is long and narrow, is situated between two massifs, the Arabo-Nubian and the geologically more recent Alpine. The ancient Arabo-Nubian massif in the south contains metal ores such as copper, iron and turquoise, and the earthquake-prone Alpine fold in the north has nonmetallic deposits such as clay, glass, sand, phosphorous, bitumen, building stone and salt. The country is also the junction of two different climates, *Mediterranean* and *desert*. The Mediterranean region had the forests which supplied fuel for domestic heating and the metal industry, and the desert had salt mines and sulfur springs (Deuteronomy 8:9). The country's geological and climatic diversity was the main motivation for the development of crafts and industry in biblical times.

Israel's geographical location made it a political nexus between Egypt and Cush in the south, and the Hittites, Assyria, Babylonia and Persia in the north.

Copper, iron ore and turquoise were located in the Arabah valley and the central Jordan Rift. The Arabah copper was first mined by the Egyptians in the thirteenth century BCE, later by King Solomon and the Judean kings. The iron deposits of the Jordan Rift, Nahal Jabbok and the Gilead mountains in Transjordan were first mined by the Philistines, then by the Judean and Israelite kings (I Kings 7:46–47).

Three categories of artisans are mentioned in the Bible: carpenters, stonemasons and metalworkers (I Chronicles 22:15–16). Carpenters and stonemasons plied their craft in much of the Mediterranean climate hill country and the Sharon coastal plain forests. The metalworkers mined ores in the Arabah, Jordan Rift, Edom and Gilead, then extracted the metal from the ore in the Sharon forests. Four materials were required: the *ore*, mined from the Nubian sandstone of the rift; *fuel*, from the rain-blessed forests of the mountains and the Sharon plain; *bellows*, made from hides and wood for the smelting fire; and a *melting pot* in a brick oven.

The production of one ton of metal, which required 25 tons of wood, was divided into two stages. First the ore, containing between one and 50 percent metal, was extracted from the sandstone by smelting fires fed by wood gathered from bushes and trees in the vicinity of the mine. Then the smelted ore was transported to a forest, and with wood- or charcoal-fueled fires was melted down into the metal from which implements were forged.

The metal industry, especially Jewish metalworking in biblical times, was more technologically advanced in the Israelite (which split from Judah in 928 BCE) than the Judean kingdom, because it had the greatest forests mentioned in the Bible—those of the Sharon plain, the Carmel range west of the Jordan, and Gilead and Bashan, in Transjordan. King Ahab (871–851 BCE) developed that industry and, according to Assyrian sources, had more chariots—2,000—than any other member of the ten- to twelve-kingdom-strong anti-Assyrian league.

Copper and bronze were used mainly for jewelry, liquid containers, cooking utensils and certain weapons and tools. Iron

## THE ANCIENT NEAR EAST — PHYSICAL

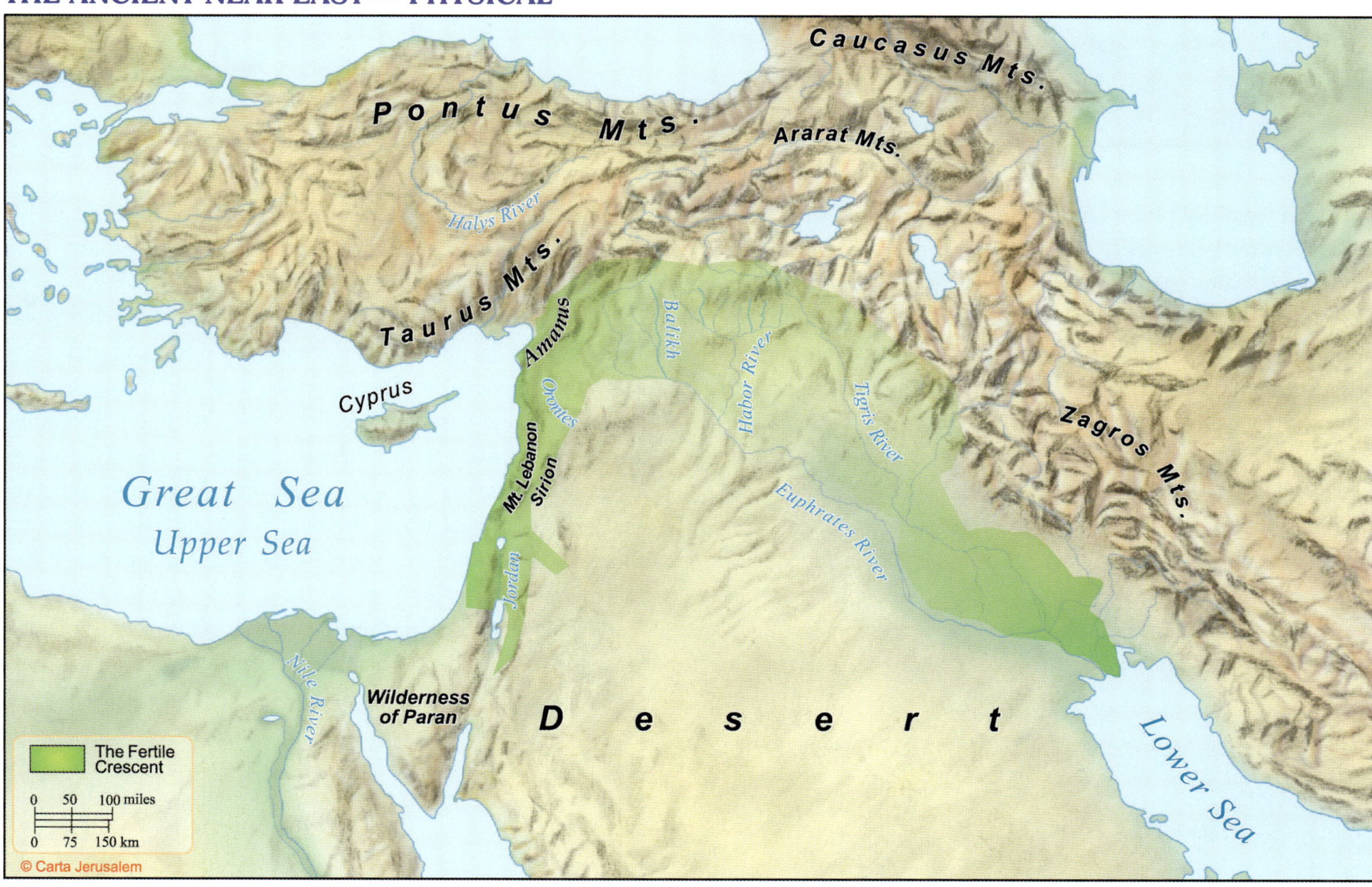

## THE ECONOMY OF THE ANCIENT NEAR EAST

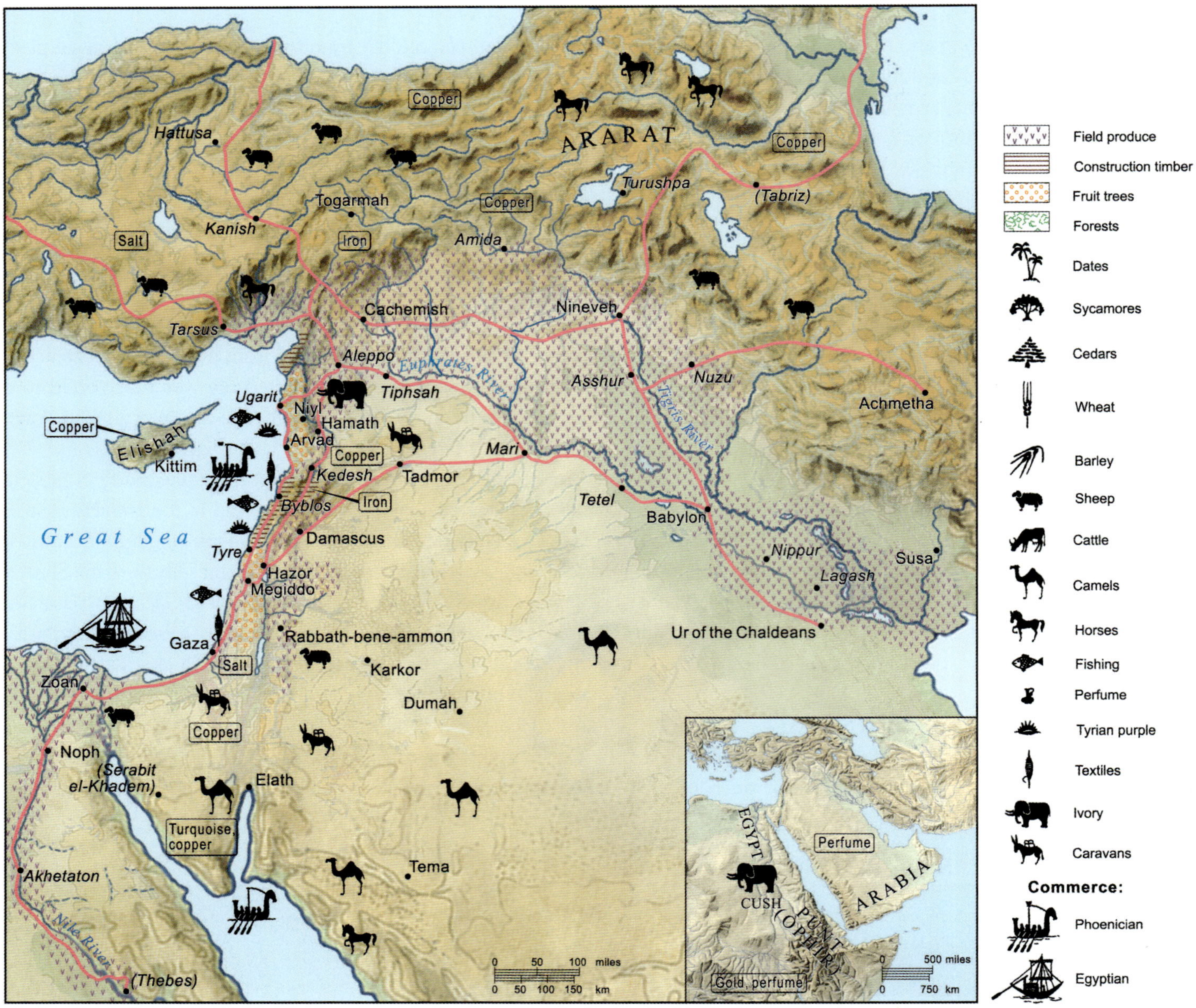


and wood were used for tools, weapons, chariots and ships.

The nonmetallic ores, which were mainly of secondary importance, were used for making clay utensils such as those for holding water and cooking. A mixture of bitumen and clay produced southwest of the Dead Sea (Isaiah 34:9) was used mainly for waterproofing ships, roofs and building foundations, cistern repair, and for export to Egypt, where it was used in mummification. The glass industry used sand from the Mediterranean beaches and from the Negeb and Edom (Job 28:17). The country's main industry was the production of salt, which was of crucial importance in food preservation and for salting the sacrificial meat. Salt produced from the sea contained harmful chemicals. But the country's best salt was produced from the pure salt stone of Mount Sodom, southwest of the 6-mile- (10-km-) long, 1.2-mile- (2-km-) wide Dead Sea (Genesis 19:26). Salt, in addition to its use in meat, fish and vegetable preservation, was used in tanning, pharmacy, and separating dross from precious metals. The finest salt was also an export commodity.

The geopolitical status of the country in biblical times, when it was situated between the powerful kingdoms of the north and south, and between the invading Sea Peoples in the west and the marauding desert tribes in the east, prompted the kings of Judah and Israel to develop the weapons and defense industries. These industries included stonemasonry for fortifying city walls and the construction of watchtowers to guard over the high, wide city gates; carpentry and metalworking for the chariot and shipbuilding industries; and metal-smithing for the weapons industry (II Kings 24:14, 16; Jeremiah 29:2). A highly developed system of weapons industries was needed because the country had to be on constant alert against enemies.

# WHO LAID THE FOUNDATIONS OF THE EARTH, THAT IT SHOULD NOT BE REMOVED FOR EVER

(Psalms 104:5)

Psalm 104 dwells on the wonders of the Creator's work. The psalm begins with the creation of the world, the stages in the formation of its landscape and the seas. It goes on to describe the water sources on land which provide for animal and plant life and the rearing of wild animals and birds. The psalm then considers the course of night and day, which influences man's labor on the land, the earth's renewal and man's seafaring endeavors on the oceans and seas.

The psalm's description of the stages in the earth's formation coincides, broadly speaking, with the Creation account in Genesis (chapter 1) and is amazingly similar to the findings of geological research. It tells of the stages in the earth's formation according to its geological and tectonic order: the raising and lowering of continents, land folding, rifts and faults and volcanic eruptions along the faults.

At the outset we find a description of the solid massifs which are the earth's foundation:

> Who laid the foundations of the earth, that it should not be removed for ever.
>
> (Psalms 104:5)

In this region the Arabo-Nubian Massif, which includes Sinai, the southern part of the Negeb, East Africa and Arabia, contains a landmass of this kind. The quote which follows describes the movements in the foundations, their raising and lowering according to God's word:

> Thou coveredst it with the deep as with a garment: the waters stood above the mountains.
>
> (Psalms 104:6)

Thus the waters of the great, ancient Thetis Sea, which flooded southern Europe and northern Africa, covered the mountain peaks of Israel, thus reducing the area of dry land. Then the pressure of gases from the depths of the earth caused the massif to rise and forced the waters to retreat to their previous location. As a result of this activity the land area expanded and the continental shelf appeared:

> At thy rebuke they fled; at the voice of thy thunder they hasted away.
>
> ...Thou hast set a bound that they may not pass over; that they turn not again to cover the earth.
>
> (Psalms 104:7, 9)

> And God said, Let the waters under the heaven be gathered together unto one place, and let the dry land appear: and it was so.
>
> (Genesis 1:9)

*"Then the channels of water were seen, and the foundations of the world were discovered at thy rebuke"* (Psalms 18:15) (photo Barry Wilmore/NASA).

The Book of Job also describes the phenomenon of raising and lowering, of the appearance and disappearance of the continental shelf:

> Where wast thou when I laid the foundations of the earth? declare if thou hast understanding.
>
> Who hath laid the measurements thereof, if thou knowest? or who hath stretched the line upon it?
>
> Whereupon are the foundations thereof fastened? or who laid the cornerstone thereof....
>
> (Job 38:4–6)

Then came the land folding which produced the anticlines and synclines, the mountains, the hills and the valleys:

> They go up by the mountains; they go down by the valleys unto the place which thou hast founded for them.
>
> (Psalms 104:8)

In the last stage, as a result of the folding, the land cracked slowly and ravines cut into the landscape:

> He sendeth the springs into the valleys; which run among the hills.
>
> (Psalms 104:10)

Then came the sudden volcanic shocks which caused basalt lava to pour out of the craters and inundate the mountains forming the plateaus:

> He looketh on the earth, and it trembleth: he toucheth the hills, and they smoke.
>
> (Psalms 104:32)

In a similar vein:

> Then the earth shook and trembled; the foundations also of the hills moved and were shaken, because he was wroth.
>
> There went up a smoke out of his nostrils, and fire out of his mouth devoured: coals were kindled by it.
>
> (Psalms 18:7–8)

A fitting description summarizing the wonders of God's work and His delights in the world is to be found in Proverbs:

> The LORD possessed me in the beginning of his way, before his works of old.
>
> I was set up from everlasting, from the beginning, or ever the earth was.
>
> When there were not depths, I was brought forth; when there were no fountains abounding with water.
>
> Before the mountains were settled, before the hills was I brought forth:
>
> While as yet he had not made the earth, nor the fields, nor the highest part of the dust of the world.
>
> When he prepared the heavens, I was there: when he set a compass upon the face of the depth:
>
> When he established the clouds above: when he strengthened the fountains of the deep:
>
> When he gave to the sea his decree, that the waters should not pass his commandment: when he appointed the foundations of the earth:
>
> Then I was by him, as one brought up with him: and I was daily his delight, rejoicing always before him;
>
> Rejoicing in the habitable part of his earth; and my delights were with the sons of men.
>
> (Proverbs 8:22–31)

## THEN THE EARTH SHOOK AND TREMBLED

(Psalms 18:7)

The Book of Psalms, more than any other book of the Bible, contains many picturesque descriptions of nature and brims with exotic scenery. The secrets of man's creation and the mysteries of heavenly phenomena are described, as are the phases in the world's formation, the varied climatic seasonal atmospheric phenomena, the growth of forests, grass and herbs, reptiles and other creatures, man's labor on the land, and the ways of sailors and ships on the open seas.

Psalm 18 provides such a vivid picture of all the stages of volcanic activity from eruption to abatement, as if the psalmist had actually stood on a mountain peak and observed every detail of the eruption. First we will describe the different stages in the course of the volcanic eruption as they are depicted in the psalm—and which are amazingly similar, from the scientific standpoint, to what happens in nature—and then we will try to explain the meaning of the biblical poet's vision.

The first stage of volcanic activity entails a powerful earthquake which sends shudders through its environment:

> Then the earth shook and trembled; the foundations also of the hills moved and were shaken, because he was wroth.
>
> (Psalms 18:7)

A terrifying earthquake such as this may cause cracks in solid rock and a burst of gases and flames to issue from the cracks and the crater:

> There went up a smoke from his nostrils, and fire out of his mouth devoured: coals were kindled by it.
>
> (Psalms 18:8)

And in Psalms 104:32:

> He looketh on the earth and it trembleth:
> he toucheth the hills, and they smoke.
>
> (Psalms 104:32)

These gases rise high in the sky, and descend alternately, thickening when they come into contact with the water vapor in the atmosphere and causing total darkness, smoke storms and the rise of volcanic ash. Finally these precipitates pour down to earth:

> He bowed the heavens also, and came down; and darkness was under his feet.
>
> And he rode upon a cherub, and did fly: yea, he did fly upon the wings of the wind.
>
> He made darkness his secret place; his pavilion round about him were dark waters and thick clouds of the skies.
>
> (Psalms 18:9–11)

*Steps of a ritual bath at Khirbet Qumran fractured in the earthquake of 31* BCE (photo Samuel Magal).

Then molten, searing lava bursts out of the volcano's crater, flowing thunderously wild and flooding everything in its wake:

> At the brightness that was before him his thick clouds passed,hail stones and coals of fires....
> Yea, he sent out his arrows, and scattered them; and he shot out lightnings, and discomfited them.
>
> (Psalms 18:12, 14)

When the volcanic eruption is at sea, the waters boil and spew above the sea, throwing up vapors and flames. A pall of smoke mixed with volcanic ash rises to the sky—then suddenly an island appears. The island diverts the rising stormy waves pushing them to great distances. These powerful waves, known as *tsunami*, rush on at a speed of more than 60 miles (100 km) an hour. This phenomenon is noted in the psalm:

> Then the channels of waters were seen, and the foundations of the world were discovered at thy rebuke, O LORD, at the blast of the breath of thy nostrils.
>
> (Psalms 18:15)

An impressive description of this phenomenon is also found in Psalm 46:

> Therefore will not we fear, though the earth be removed, and though the mountains be carried into the midst of the sea;
> Though the waters thereof roar and be troubled, though the mountains shake with the swelling thereof.
>
> (Psalms 46:2–3)

After contemplating this vivid and elaborate description of volcanic activity the question arises: where was the psalmist that he could describe all the stages in the volcanic eruption in such a scientifically exact, elaborate and brilliant manner? After all, if volcanic eruptions occurred in Israel tens of thousands of years ago, what were the sources upon which the biblical poet based his visions?

After the Six-Day War, geological surveys of the basalt deposits on the Golan Heights uncovered a flock of charred goats which, according to carbon-14 tests, had perished in an eruption of lava which took place four thousand years ago—in historical time. The psalmist, it seems, was a witness to the eruption and he described its awful wonders with dramatic and enchanting exactitude.

# THE MOUNTAINS AND STREAMS OF THE LAND OF ISRAEL

# THE WATERS THEREOF ROAR AND BE TROUBLED

(Psalms 46:3)

The Book of Psalms describes Israel's lively scenes in poetry and prose with consummate artistry. The psalms praise God, the Creator of heaven, earth and man. The psalmist stands in awe while beholding a universe created with such wisdom and intelligence. The Book of Psalms has detailed descriptions of the climate, the diverse physical landscape, the plethora of lovely flora and the variety of exotic animals. One can feel how the land is renewed and provides for all of God's creatures. There are descriptions of dry, sirocco-smitten deserts where springs gush forth from the ground and turn the desert into a lake and the dry land into a fountain. There are descriptions of afforested areas where birds nest and streams of pure water sate the wild beasts. There are pictures of broad expanses of land where the furrows of the grassy fields are saturated with droplets of dew and the valleys covered with grain, and we can visualize the vines and olive trees. Mountainous areas are depicted where the wild goats and buck roam and where the rocks provide shelter for the rock-badgers. And we have the deep waters full of fish and the whale (Leviathan) and merchant ships which ply the oceans. On the whole, we are presented with a tranquil, calm pastoral scene, full of love for the natural landscape and man's works and a longing for God's creation.

Despite these ideal, tranquil scenes the Psalms also describe horrible natural disasters which are represented as God's anger unfurled, such as the volcanic eruptions on land and sea described in Psalm 46. An earthquake which topples all existing things is described by Isaiah:

> The earth is utterly broken down, the earth is clean dissolved, the earth is moved exceedingly.
>
> The earth shall reel to and fro like a drunkard, and shall be removed like a cottage; and the transgression thereof shall be heavy upon it; and it shall fall, and not rise again.
>
> (Isaiah 24:19–20)

An elaborate and astounding description of an earthquake is described in Psalm 18:

> Then the earth shook and trembled; the foundations also of the hills moved and were shaken, because he was wroth.
>
> There went up a smoke out of his nostrils, and fire out of his mouth devoured: coals were kindled by it.
>
> (Psalms 18:7–8)

Psalm 46 describes a shocking natural disaster which occurred when a volcano erupted in the midst of the sea:

> Therefore will not we fear, though the earth be removed, and though the mountains be carried into the midst of the sea;
>
> Though the waters thereof roar and be troubled, though the mountains shake with the swelling thereof.
>
> (Psalms 46:2–3)

How, then, does such a disaster happen at sea and what are the results?

In August 1883, there were a series of volcanic eruptions on the island of Krakatau, which is situated between Java and Sumatra in Southeast Asia. The big island was smashed and most of it sunk into the sea—a situation similar to that described in Psalm 46:

> ...though the earth be removed, and though the mountains be carried into the midst of the sea.
>
> (Psalms 46:2)

The Krakatau earthquake was accompanied by an earsplitting noise which was heard 3,100 miles (5,000 km) away. Volcanic matter rose to a height of 17 miles (27 km), strewing destruction in the nearby countries—compare this with the psalm:

> The heathen raged, the kingdoms were moved: he uttered his voice, the earth melted.
>
> (Psalms 46:6)

And:

> The LORD also thundered in the heavens, and the Highest gave his voice; hail stones and coals of fire.
>
> (Psalms 18:13)

But the ultimate catastrophe and destruction were caused by the rushing waves pushed on by the enormous force of the underwater eruption:

> The waters thereof roar and be troubled....
>
> (Psalms 46:3)

These waves are enormous bodies of water which rush about especially at the water's edge. Indeed at Krakatau there were waves 100 to 130 feet (30 to 40 m) high and 100 miles (160 km) in length, rushing ahead at a speed of more than 400 miles (640 km) an hour. The powerful floods caused by the reddish waters destroyed about a thousand coastal villages in Java and Sumatra, killing 36,000 people. The force of the *tsunami* hurled a boat which was 1.5 miles (2.5 km) away from the disaster to a height of 33 feet (10 m) above the land.

Compare:

> Then the channels of waters were seen, and the foundations of the world were discovered at thy rebuke, O LORD, at the blast of the breath of thy nostrils.
>
> (Psalms 18:15)

It seems that "its waters...be troubled (*yehmeru*)" refers not just to the storm but to the reddish (*hamer*) color of the waters. The Krakatau eruption caused the downpour of reddish volcanic dust on ships 1,600 miles (2,600 km) away from the eruption for three days afterwards.

*The Sea of Galilee during a storm* (photo Paul H. Wright).

# THE MOUNTAIN FALLING COMETH TO NOUGHT, AND THE ROCK IS REMOVED OUT OF HIS PLACE

(Job 14:18)

Job describes the brief life of man, the plant's longer life and the eternalness of the mountain as dependent on God's power. His view of man is pessimistic:

> Man that is born of a woman is of few days, and full of trouble.
> He cometh forth like a flower, and is cut down: he fleeth also as a shadow, and continueth not.
>
> (Job 14:1–2)

The tree, on the other hand, appears to be dead even when the potentiality of life still exists:

> For there is hope of a tree, if it be cut down, that it will sprout again, and that the tender branch thereof will not cease.
> Though the root thereof wax old in the earth, and the stock thereof die in the ground;
> Yet through the scent of water it will bud, and bring forth boughs like a plant.
>
> (Job 14:7–9)

After describing God's living creation Job turns to mighty inanimate nature, that which symbolizes eternalness. If this cannot withstand God's power what hope is there for man and flora?

Some questions are raised by Job 14:

1. In which geological structures do mountains crumble and tumble down?

2. What is the connection between tumbling mountains and the dust of the earth?

3. What is the meaning of "thou destroyest the hope of man" (Job 14:19)?

There is reason to believe that Job lived in Edom where the mountains consist of a top layer of limestone, under which lies crumbly sandstone with a durable igneous rock base. When rains pour down on such a geological formation, deep wedges are cut into the crumbly sandstone loosening great chunks of the limestone upper stratum. The same holds true for the Negeb craters. Referring to this phenomenon Job states:

> The mountain falling cometh to nought, and the rock is removed out of his place.
>
> (Job 14:18)

The erosion is compounded by the mountains' steep incline and the soil erosion is worsened by the crumbling mountains and displaced rock. In the desert, where the soil does not renew itself as easily as in more rainy areas, the result is disastrous:

> ...a sweeping rain which leaveth no food.
>
> (Proverbs 28:3)

Thus, "Thou destroyest the hope of man."

> The waters wear the stones; thou washest away the things which grow out of the dust of the earth; and thou destroyest the hope of man.
>
> (Job 14:19)

As stated, the rains loosen the stone causing it to fall away. As for the wood it seems to us that "thou washest away the things which grow out of the dust of the earth" refers to the washing away of grains *and* vegetables and trees. Most researchers, confounding the Hebrew *sefiheha*, which refers to the *objects* washed away by the floods with *sehifeha*, erosion, have interpreted the verse as meaning soil erosion. The correct interpretation seems to be that offered by Mishnah *Shevi'it* (9:1) and Talmud *Ta'anit* (19). The floods and falling rocks uproot and destroy the trees while the widespread soil erosion in Edom destroys man's food. When this threefold disaster strikes the land, people are forced to uproot their homes and move elsewhere:

> His confidence shall be rooted out of his tabernacle, and it shall bring him to the king of terrors.
>
> (Job 18:14)

Thus three of God's creations are involved:

1. Man, who by his very nature wanders, carrying his belongings with him:

> The flood breaketh out from the inhabitant; even the waters forgotten of the foot: they are dried up, they are gone away from men.
>
> (Job 28:4)

2. The trees of the field which are more steadfast uniting soil and rock and imbuing man with hope—

> For there is hope of a tree....
>
> (Job 14:7)

But since trees bind man to his soil—

> ...mine hope hath he removed like a tree.
>
> (Job 19:10)

3. The uprooting of stone, the symbol of permanence, spells disaster for man, his land and its fruits. Thus—

> Thou destroyest the hope of man.
>
> (Job 14:19)

# STONE, ROCK AND FLINT [*ZUR*]

(Deuteronomy 32:13)

The uses of stone were manifold in Bible times; it was used by shepherds, farmers, miners, builders and craftsmen, as well as for the manufacture of tools and weapons. Rock and flint symbolized strength and fortitude, synonymous with the Deity, and provided man with shelter and watchposts. The strong, sharp flintstones were used to make tools such as axes, hammers and chisels, and weapons such as Joshua's flint swords, with which he circumcised the Israelites (Joshua 5:2–3), or as we find in Psalms:

> Thou hast turned back the edge [*zur*] of his sword, and thou hast not made him stand in battle.
>
> (Psalms 89:43)

They were also used to make slingstones together with bows and arrows, as stated in Job 41:28:

> The arrow cannot make him flee: slingstones are turned with him into stubble.

Or as we find in the narrative of David's fight with Goliath (I Samuel 17:40). Shepherds rolled a stone over the opening of the well, to ensure their tribal ownership over the well, as we find in Genesis 29:2–3:

> ...for out of that well they watered the flocks: and a great stone was upon the well's mouth. And thither were all the flocks gathered: and they rolled the stone from the well's mouth, and watered the sheep, and put the stone again upon the well's mouth in his place.
>
> (Genesis 29:2–3)

The settlers used stone for the construction of houses (Psalms 118:22), and for the Temple and other ornamental houses, as we find in II Kings 12:12:

> And to masons, and hewers of stone, and to buy timber and hewed stone to repair the breaches of the house of the LORD, and for all that was laid out for the house to repair it.
>
> (II Kings 12:12; see also II Kings 22:6)

The farmers built their fences from stone, constructing agricultural terraces on the mountain slopes, as we find in the parable of the vineyard in Isaiah 5:2:

> And he fenced it, and gathered out the stones thereof, and planted it with the choicest vine, and built a tower in the midst of it, and also made a winepress therein.
>
> (Isaiah 5:2)

The mountain vineyards were based on terraces and stone fences, as related in the description of the vineyards in the war against Moab in II Kings 3:19 and 3:25:

> And ye shall smite every fenced city, and every choice city, and shall fell every good tree, and stop up all wells of water, and mar every good piece of land with stones....
>
> And they beat down the cities, and on every good piece of land cast every man his stone, and filled it ... only in Kir-haraseth left they the stones thereof.
>
> (II Kings 3:19, 3:25)

The rocks were exploited for their metal ores which were the raw materials of industry, as described in Deuteronomy 8:9:

> a land whose stones are iron, and out of whose hills thou mayest dig brass.

The descendants of Kenaz were craftsmen, who dwelt in Edom, as we find in I Chronicles 4:14:

> and Seraiah begat Joab, the father of the valley of Charashim; for they were craftsmen [*harashim*].
>
> (I Chronicles 4:14)

The metal tools were forged near the mines in the mountains of Gilead, as told of Solomon in I Kings 7:46:

> In the plain of Jordan did the king cast them, in the clay ground between Succoth and Zarthan.
>
> (I Kings 7:46)

The basic rocks and sandstones were exploited for their precious stones, and the Israelites embedded the High Priest's breastplate with twelve types of precious stone, one for each of the twelve tribes:

> a sardius, a topaz, and a carbuncle ... an emerald, a sapphire, and a diamond ... a ligure, an agate, and an amethyst ... a beryl, and an onyx, and a jasper.
>
> (Exodus 28:17–20)

Stone mounds were built by the ancients and served as border markers in the fields and on the tribal boundaries, as well as on mountain tops, hilltops and along routeways, where they served as monuments, pillars and ritual objects. These mounds of stones symbolized the existence of a treaty or covenant, and served as landmarks for the traveler, as we find in Genesis 31:46–47:

> And Jacob said unto his brethren, Gather stones; and they took stones, and made an heap; and they did eat there upon the heap. And Laban called it Jegar-sahadutha: but Jacob called it Galeed.
>
> (Genesis 31:46–47)

The eternal Rock and Crag were synonyms for the Deity, symbolizing fortitude, stability and strength, as stated in Isaiah:

> The Lord is exalted; for he dwelleth on high....
>
> (Isaiah 33:5)

since the high mountain peaks were dedicated as shrines. God was given eight synonymous names which signified high-rising, stable rock: *sela* (rock), *zur* (crag), *misgav* (fortress), *mezudah* (fort), *maoz* (fort), *magen* (shield), *keren-yesha* (mighty champion), *miphlat* (deliverer), as we find in David's prayer of thanksgiving in II Samuel 22:2–3:

> The Lord is my rock [*sal'i*], and my fortress [*mezudati*], and my deliverer [*miphlati*];
>
> The God of my rock; in him will I trust: he is my shield, and the horn of my salvation, my high tower, and my refuge, my savior; thou savest me from violence.
>
> (II Samuel 22:2–3; see also Deuteronomy 32:4, 32:15, 32:30–31; Isaiah 17:10, 51:1; Psalms 21:3, 42:9, 62:7)

Man and beast found shelter in the caves and crevices of the

*"A land whose stones are iron"* (Deuteronomy 8:9) (photo Samuel Magal).

cliffs, as we find in Numbers 24:21 with reference to the Kenites:

Strong is thy dwelling place,
and thou puttest thy nest in a rock.

(Numbers 24:21)

And in Isaiah 7:19, describing the army of Assyria:

They shall come, and shall rest all of them in the desolate valleys, and in the holes of the rocks.

(Isaiah 7:19; see also Jeremiah 48:28 on Moab)

I Samuel 13:6 tells of the refuge sought in the rocks by the Benjaminites during their war with the Philistines:

When the men of Israel saw that they were in a strait (for the people were distressed), then the people did hide themselves in caves, and in thickets and in rocks and in high places, and in pits.

(I Samuel 13:6; see also Isaiah 2:19)

Animals such as wild goats, badgers and doves also took refuge in the rocks:

The high hills are a refuge for the wild goats; and the rocks for the conies.

(Psalms 104:18; see also Proverbs 30:26)

And the Song of Songs 2:14 states:

O my dove, that art in the clefts of the rock.

(Song of Songs 2:14; see also Jeremiah 48:28)

Job, on the other hand, describes the eagle as:

She dwelleth and abideth on the rock, upon the crag of the rock, and the strong place.

(Job 39:28)

The rock precipices and mountain tops were points of orientation in the field and the wilderness, as we find in the narrative of Jonathan and his arms bearer:

And between the passages, by which Jonathan sought to go over unto the Philistines' garrison, there was a sharp rock on the one side and a sharp rock on the other side; and the name of the one was Bozez, and the name of the other Seneh.

(I Samuel 14:4)

The Israelites followed Samson down "to the top of the rock Etam" (Judges 15:11), and David fleeing from Saul went "down into a rock, and abode in the wilderness of Maon" (I Samuel 23:25).

The rock which provided shade in summer for man and beast is mentioned in Isaiah 32:2:

A man shall be as a hiding place from the wind, and a covert from the tempest; as rivers of water in a dry place, as the shadow of a great rock in a weary land.

(Isaiah 32:2)

The rock was also a source of water and the basis for the formation of soil for agricultural purposes, as we find in the narrative of Moses and the miracle of the rock (Numbers 20:11):

And Moses lifted up his hand, and with his rod smote the rock twice: and the water came out abundantly, and the congregation drank, and their beasts also.

(Numbers 20:11; see also Isaiah 48:21; Psalms 78:16, 114:8; Nehemiah 9:15)

Deuteronomy 32:13 describes the agriculture:

He made him to suck honey out of the rock, and oil out of the flinty rock.

(Deuteronomy 32:13)

Similarly, we find in Psalms 81:16:

He should have fed them also with the finest of the wheat: and
with honey out of the rock should I have satisfied thee.

(Psalms 81:16)

How then, were honey and oil extracted from the rock? In analyzing mountain agriculture there appear to be two explanations to these passages: (a) The vineyards were planted on the hard rocky mountains, and the vine symbolizes honey obtained from the raisins, whereas the olive was grown on the soft rock in the hills, and this is the origin of the oil. (b) The rocks of the mountains were used to hew out winepresses and oil presses, as we find in Joel 2:24:

And the floors shall be full of wheat, and the fats shall overflow with wine and oil.

(Joel 2:24; see also Joel 4:13)

Thus the wine vats symbolize the honey from the raisins, and the oil presses the oil produced from pressure of the rock. Job 19:23–24 mentions the use of a rock for engraving as were the words of the Law:

Oh that my words were now written! oh that they were printed in a book!

That they were graven with an iron pen and lead in the rock for ever!

(Job 19:23–24)

# IF I HAVE MADE GOLD MY HOPE, OR HAVE SAID TO THE FINE GOLD, THOU ART MY CONFIDENCE

(Job 31:24)

Edom might have produced abundant quantities of food but was also blessed with the riches buried beneath its soil. Beneath the limestone layers of Edom are several hundred feet of sandstone and granite which contain precious stones, copper, iron and gold and the other ores of Mount Seir.

The copper mines discovered by Nelson Glueck in Punon—in Edom's Ge-haharashim—were, according to Glueck, the most extensive and significant in the entire Arabah. Punon is noted as the site where Moses fashioned the bronze serpent (Numbers 21:9, 33:43). Ge-haharashim (Valley of the Craftsmen), according to S. Abramsky, was an important Kenite and Kenizite industrial center (see I Chronicles 4:14).

The Book of Job notes the deposits of iron, copper and gold in Edom:

Surely there is a vein for the silver,
and a place for gold where they fine it.
Iron is taken out of the earth,
and [copper] is molten out of the stone.

(Job 28:1–2)

Then shalt thou lay up gold as dust,
and the gold of Ophir as the stones of the brooks.

(Job 22:24)

Glass was produced from Edom's sandstone and gold:

The gold and the crystal cannot equal it: and the exchange of it shall not be for jewels of fine gold.

(Job 28:17)

Other passages also hint at Edom's natural resources:

He shall flee from the iron weapon, and the bow of steel shall strike him through.

(Job 20:24)

His bones are as strong pieces of brass; his bones are like bars of iron.

(Job 40:18)

Edom's natural resources supported flourishing weapons and jewelry industries. Thus the territory was a bone of contention between Edom and Judah. The wars of David for control of Edom are recounted in I Chronicles (I Chronicles 18:12–13) and in the following passage from II Samuel:

And David gat him a name when he returned from smiting of the Syrians in the valley of salt, being eighteen thousand men. And he put garrisons in Edom; throughout all Edom put he garrisons, and all they of Edom became David's servants. And the LORD preserved David whithersoever he went.

(II Samuel 8:13–14)

Solomon's great wealth was due in part to the exploitation of the Edomite and Arabah mines and his control of the trade routes. Solomon also controlled the port of Elath and the nearby Ezion-geber. Amaziah, king of Judah, fought the Edomites (II Chronicles 25:11–12) as did Alexander Yannai, who fought the Nabatean inhabitants of Edom during the time of the Second Temple.

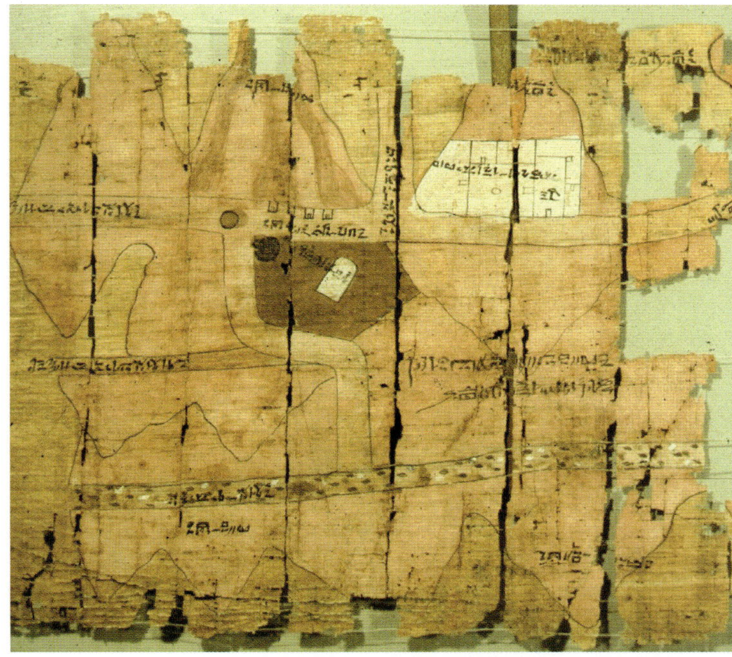

*Egyptian map describing the gold mines in Wadi Hammamat, 12th century BCE* (public domain, via Wikimedia Commons).

Ezekiel testifies to Edom's importance as a major crossroad for the caravans dealing in precious stones and metals:

Dedan was thy merchant in precious clothes for chariots. Arabia, and all the princes of Kedar, they occupied with thee in lambs, and rams, and goats: in these were they thy merchants. The merchants of Sheba and Raamah, they were thy merchants: they occupied in thy fairs with chief of all spices, and with all precious stones, and gold.

(Ezekiel 27:20–22; see also Isaiah 60:6; Jeremiah 6:20)

Thus, in addition to the raw materials which came from Edom, or which passed through Edom in caravans, there were the fragrant spices and perfumes which came from the gardens of Arabia and Yemen:

Awake, O north wind;
and come, thou south;
blow upon my garden,
that the spices thereof may flow out.
Let my beloved come into his garden,
and eat his pleasant fruits.

(Song of Songs 4:16)

The merchants apparently dealt in the pearls which were gathered in the Gulf of Elath:

No mention shall be made of coral, or of pearls: for the price of wisdom is above rubies.

(Job 28:18)

# IRON IS TAKEN OUT OF THE EARTH, AND COPPER IS MOLTEN OUT OF THE STONE

(Job 28:2)

*Assyrian siege-engine attacking the city wall of Lachish. Detail of relief from Sennacherib's Southwest Palace at Nineveh, currently housed in the British Museum, London* (photo Osama Shukir Muhammed Amin FRCP[Glasg], via Wikimedia Commons).

Were iron and copper ores mined in Israel and worked there or were they imported? Judging by biblical and extra-biblical sources, archaeological evidence and the geological structure of the country's stone, it is probable that copper and iron ores were mined in Israel. Clear biblical proof is to be found in Deuteronomy:

> a land whose stones are iron, and out of whose hills thou mayest dig [copper].
>
> (Deuteronomy 8:9)

The Book of Job mentions the ores, forging iron and copper implements in a number of passages.

The ore is mentioned in Job 22:24:

> Then shalt thou lay up gold as … [ore].
>
> (Job 22:24)

The smelting is noted in Job 38:38:

> When the dust [ore] groweth into hardness, and the clods cleave fast together.
>
> (Job 38:38)

The strength and resilience of the metals are noted in chapter 40:18:

> His bones are as strong pieces of brass, his bones are like bars of iron.
>
> (Job 40:18)

And the metal weapons in chapter 20:24:

> He shall flee from the iron weapon, and the bow of steel shall strike him through.
>
> (Job 20:24)

Let us look for the iron and copper mines, evidence of mining and the smelting and forging processes.

It is clear today both from the country's geological structure and the archaeological evidence that copper ore was mined at a number of locations in the Arabah valley from the time of the ancient Egyptians through the days of the Jewish kings and the Roman and Byzantine periods. Iron ore was discovered in Wadi es-Sabra, southeast of Petra in Edom, and in Nahal Jabbok from the time of the first Jewish kings intermittently until Ottoman times.

As Josephus (4.8.2) notes in the *Jewish Wars*:

> There is a mountain in this country called the Mount of Iron which stretches until the Land of Moab.
>
> (*Wars* 4.8.2)

Josephus was probably referring to Nahal Jabbok. When the Mishnah (*Succah* 4:4) states that the dates of "iron" may be eaten, it is probably referring to the dates which grew in the area of the Mount of Iron mentioned by Josephus.

Nelson Glueck has written about the dross of the Nahal Jabbok used by the inhabitants of Ajloun, north of Jabbok, to pave the roads against the winter mud, 2 miles (3 km) on either side.

The ancients produced the huge quantities of coal required in ironworking from the expanses of the Gilead forests to the north and south of the Jabbok ravine. Solomon exploited the natural advantages of the Jabbok and Gilead ravines for producing iron and bronze for his Temple:

> In the plain of the Jordan did the king cast them, in the clay ground between Succoth and Zarthan.
>
> (I Kings 7:46)

Further evidence that Solomon was engaged in extensive mining operations is found in his request to Hiram:

> Send me now therefore a man cunning to work in gold, and in silver, and in brass, and in iron....
>
> (II Chronicles 2:7)

In ancient times a concerted effort was made to ensure independence in the exploitation of raw materials and manufacture—especially in the arms and chariot industries. Thus Joash, who fortified the Temple, the foremost bastion of the city:

> And the king and Jehoiada gave it to such as did the work of the service of the house of the LORD, and hired masons and carpenters to repair the house of the LORD, and also such as wrought iron and brass to mend the house of the LORD.
>
> (II Chronicles 24:12)

The chief instrument of war in ancient times was the armored chariot. They often swayed the battle and can be compared to the armored corps which make up the backbone of modern armies. It is a fair assumption that Solomon was the first Israelite king to develop the armored vehicle industry.

> And Solomon gathered together chariots and horsemen: and he had a thousand and four hundred chariots, and twelve thousand horsemen, whom he bestowed in the cities for chariots, and with the king at Jerusalem.
>
> (I Kings 10:26)

II Chronicles states that "Solomon had four thousand stalls for horses and chariots" (II Chronicles 9:25). The kings of Judah and Israel, especially Ahab, followed Solomon's example. When he allied himself with the Aramean kings against the Assyrians at Qarqar, Ahab, according to the Shalmaneser inscription, had two thousand war vehicles. By emphasizing metal forging—

*Bronze helmet, late 7th century BCE* (public domain; gift of Norbert Schimmel Trust, 1989, currently housed in the Metropolitan Museum of Art).

> Iron is taken out of the earth, and [copper] is molten out of the stone.
>
> (Job 28:2)

Job bears witness to the iron industry of his day. Metalwork was most probably conducted in Edom and in Gilead, continuing the sovereign Jewish kingdom's tradition of an autarchic arms industry.

*Jabbok River (Nahr ez-Zarqa)* (photo Jim Greenhill, U.S. Army [public domain], via Wikimedia Commons).

# THE SMITH THAT BLOWETH THE COALS IN THE FIRE

(Isaiah 54:16)

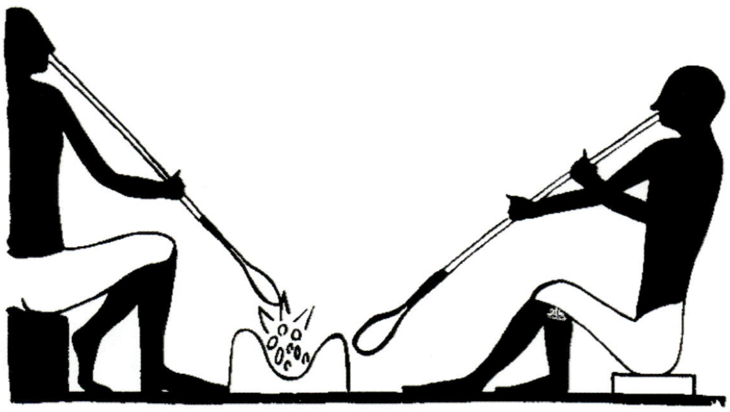

*Two smiths blowing into a fire (19th century BCE).*

Isaiah mentions two important industrial raw materials, which are needed in industry, iron and coal:

> Behold, I have created the smith that bloweth the coals in the fire, and that bringeth forth an instrument for his work; and I have created the waster to destroy.

And:

> The smith with the tongs both worketh in the coals, and fashioneth it with hammers, and worketh it with the strength of his arms.
>
> (Isaiah 44:12)

We will examine the importance of wood and iron in the life of the ancients, and the sources of wood and iron ore. We will then attempt to locate the vicinity where the first iron workers mined their ore.

Primordial man used the wood of the country's forests for fire. Fire served to lengthen his life-span by heating his dwelling and cooking his food. The campfire provided the setting for the development of social life and its light provided prehistoric man with a sense of security at night. Signal fires were the means of communication by night and day. Primordial man learned how to use wood for other purposes after he learned how to feed the fire. He went on to build the wooden plow, the shaft, the wheel and the cart, and learned how to fashion the boat. Man was encouraged by the fire to cook his food and then he slowly learned how to smelt metals in fire. Throughout history, fuel has been a crucial commodity and regardless of his cultural level, man has transported fuels more than any other commodity over great distances and in enormous quantities.

The smelting of metals and the manufacture of metal implements caused momentous changes in thinking in ancient times and revolutionized human history. War materiel was fashioned from metals and later on advanced work tools and chariots. Metal implements provided nations with the economic basis of their existence and helped bring about mass industry. Ancient Eastern rulers as well as modern powers traveled hundreds and thousands of miles to produce metals and powerful nations fought in order to

*Nahal Jabbok (Nahr ez-Zarqa).* (photo Adeeb Atwan, via Wikimedia Commons)

*Egyptian wall painting of artisans at work (first half of 14th century BCE)* (photo Kingn8link, via Wikimedia Commons).

control the sources of metal ores.

As to the country's sources of iron ore and wood and in light of our biblical verse, "the smith that bloweth the coals in the fire," it is necessary to dwell on the meaning of the term "smith." In biblical terms, a smith is a craftsman who works in stone, wood or metal. It is important to note that neither the mason nor the carpenter needs the materials of the other's specialty. Stone can be cut without using wood and wood can be crafted without the use of stone. But the smith must use wood in melting or forging metal. Moreover, the quantity of wood needed for preparing the smith's coals is more than twenty times the quantity of the metal being produced. Though it is convenient if the metal ore and the forests are located near each other, throughout history fuels have been transported to the mines.

Two ancient iron mines have been discovered in the country, one in Wadi es-Sabra, approximately 4 miles (7 km) southwest of Petra and the other in Nahal Jabbok, south of the village of Ajloun, where enormous quantities of dross have been found. The Wadi es-Sabra mines, which were discovered by Nelson Glueck, contain 63 percent iron. Both of these mines are in close proximity to the forests which supplied the wood for charcoal. In the mountains of Edom, at altitudes varying between 3,280 and 5,250 feet (1,000 and 1,600 m) above sea level, there is a forest of junipers that reach a height of 33 feet (10 m), and oak. In the Gilead, where Nahal Jabbok is located, there are oak and pine forests.

Now to the question of the smiths and where they produced their ore. Most scholars, basing their hypotheses on scriptural references, believe that the Philistines brought ironcraft with them from Asia Minor:

> Now there was no smith found throughout all the land of Israel: for the Philistines said, Lest the Hebrews make them swords or spears: But all the Israelites went down to the Philistines, to sharpen every man his share, and his coulter, and his axe, and his mattock.
>
> (I Samuel 13:19–20)

According to R. J. Forbes, the foremost expert on ancient Near Eastern metallurgy, the Philistines imported iron ore from Anatolia to be forged and worked here. Forbes's conclusion is unacceptable for three reasons:

1. Furnaces for forging iron which date from the twelfth to the tenth centuries BCE have been found in the tels of Nahal Jabbok;
2. During Solomon's time Nahal Jabbok was the greatest iron manufacturing center in Israel;
3. Solomon, who appointed twelve ministers to administer the country, appointed three economic ministers in Gilead alone, one of whom hailed from Mahanaim, which was apparently the center of the copper and iron industry:

> Geber the son of Uri was in the country of Gilead....
>
> The son of Geber, in Ramoth-gilead; to him pertained the towns of Jair the son of Manasseh, which are in Gilead; to him also pertained the region of Argob, which is in Bashan, threescore great cities with walls and brasen bars: Ahinadab the son of Iddo had Mahanaim.
>
> (I Kings 4:19, 4:13–14)

Thus it seems that at Nahal Jabbok there was:

> ...the smith that bloweth the coals in the fire, and that bringeth forth an instrument for his work.
>
> (Isaiah 54:16)

# GE-HAHARASHIM

(Nehemiah 11:35)

*Tabor oak* (photo Paul H. Wright).

Ge-haharashim (Valley of the Craftsmen) is mentioned twice in the Bible: "Lod, Ono, Ge-haharashim" (Nehemiah 11:35) and—

> And the sons of Kenaz; Othniel, and Seraiah: and the sons of Othniel; Hathath. And Meonothai begat Ophrah: and Seraiah begat Joab, the father of the valley of Charashim; for they were craftsmen.
>
> (I Chronicles 4:13–14)

The verse emphasizes the occupation of the Kenizzites: "for they were craftsmen." Along with the Kenites the Kenizzites lived in the Negeb and the Arabah. Nelson Glueck found evidence of ancient iron and copper mining in the Arabah rift and in the foothills of Mount Edom. One of the valleys in the vicinity is known in Arabic as Wadi Nehas which means valley of copper (in Hebrew, copper is called *nehosheth*). Its Hebrew name was probably Ge-harashim. The location of the site in the Arabah is a likely assumption but why was there a Ge-haharashim in the Lod and Ono valley? Furthermore, why the definite article in Ge-*ha*harashim—*the* Valley of the Craftsmen?

It is important to note the Ge-haharashim which is mentioned along with Lod and Ono among the other cities where the former Babylonian exiles settled is in the tribal inheritance of Benjamin. Professor Benjamin Mazar writes in the Hebrew *Biblical Encyclopedia* that the Benjaminites settled the area in First Temple times. What then is the connection between the tribe of Benjamin and metal craftsmen? Even more curious is the fact that the decisive battle between the House of Saul and the Philistines took place in the insignificant Michmash, in eastern Benjamin and not in Gibeah or Ramah or one of Saul's other important cities. It seems to us that the battle was not fought over Michmash alone but for control of the road leading from Michmash to the Jordan Rift and Jabbok where the iron mines were located. It is necessary to associate the wars between the Israelite tribes and the Philistines in Shiloh, where a road leading to Jabbok emanates, with the Philistine hold over Beth-shean and the iron mines of Jabbok.

The First Book of Kings mentions the copper vessels for Solomon's Temple which were fashioned in Nahal Jabbok:

> In the plain of Jordan did the king cast them, in the clay ground between Succoth and Zarthan.
>
> (I Kings 7:46)

Sure enough, in the Tell Deir Alla dig furnaces and smelting pots for copper, tuyères and dross were discovered from the Early and Middle Iron ages. It seems likely that the task of the special administrator appointed by Solomon at Mahanaim, in Nahal Jabbok, was to oversee the production and smelting of iron.

W. F. Albright, writing about the Philistines in the *Biblical Encyclopedia*, notes that the script on the clay tablets found at Tell Deir Alla, which is in Jabbok, is Minoan, i.e., the language of the Sea Peoples.

Thus the Philistines, who had a monopoly over the country's ironworks, were probably trying to wrest Michmash away from Saul, in order to get at the iron ore in Jabbok and transport it via the land of Benjamin to Ge-haharashim in the Lod and Ono valley.

The main occupation of the Philistine craftsmen was ironworking:

> Now there was no smith found throughout all the land of Israel; for the Philistines said, Lest the Hebrews make them swords or spears: But all the Israelites went down to the Philistines, to sharpen every man his share, and his coulter, and his axe, and his mattock.
>
> (I Samuel 13:19–20)

And:

> The garrison of the Philistines went out to the passage of Michmash.
>
> (I Samuel 13:23)

The Jerusalem Talmud 43:1, *halakhah* 1, notes that "Lod and Ono were Ge-haharashim." Professor Mazar, however, ventures that Zerifin was the Ge-haharashim of talmudic times because it might have been the site of *Zerifat* (=refining) metals.

During biblical times and in particular the time of the Second Temple, the Sharon plain was covered by a dense oak forest which provided the fuel for the iron foundries. This thick forest is mentioned in the records of the Egyptian pharaohs' campaigns in Canaan, by Josephus and in Byzantine and Crusader records. Only a hint of its erstwhile grandeur remains in the forest near Karkour today.

The excavations of Benjamin and Amihai Mazar at Tell Qasile uncovered a large Philistine temple, evidence of the Philistine control over the ancient oak forest which stretched from the Yarkon River to Lod and Ono. The tributaries of the Yarkon River ran along that route, one of which apparently was alongside Ge-haharashim. Thus the Philistines tried to conquer the Benjaminite country which had the iron mines near Nahal Jabbok in the vicinity of Mahanaim (the capital of Mephibosheth, Saul's son) on the east and Ge-haharashim, the center of the ironworks on the west.

In summation, the smelting of the iron ore took place near the iron mines of Nahal Jabbok where there was an ample supply of wood and the foundries were at Ge-haharashim in Sharon, in the midst of the Tabor oak forest and the center of the Philistine settlement.

## THE CRAFTSMEN [*HARASH*] AND SMITHS [*MASGER*]

(II Kings 24:14)

Before dealing with the occupations of the craftsmen and smiths and where they worked, let us discuss the meaning of the two terms. A craftsman is an artisan who works in either wood, stone, copper or iron. As David instructed Solomon on the building of the Temple:

> There are workmen with thee in abundance, hewers and workers of stone and timber, and all manner of cunning men for every manner of work. Of the gold, the silver, and the brass, and the iron, there is no number.
>
> (I Chronicles 22:15–16)

Eliezer Ben-Yehuda, the pioneer of modern Hebrew lexicography, defined smith (*masger*) as "a kind of lock with which to close (*lisgor*) something." The reference, however, seems to be to an artisan who constructs an iron or brass partition enclosing the courtyard and the house, the gate and the latticework in order to strengthen the structure. As is written in II Chronicles:

> ...and hired masons and carpenters to repair the house of the LORD, and also such as wrought iron and brass to mend the house of the LORD.
>
> (II Chronicles 24:12)

Smiths also engaged in fashioning iron weapons such as swords, spears, javelins, lances, hatchets, machetes, knives, missiles and battering rams.

Copper crafts were probably introduced into the country by non-Israelites, such as the Kenites and Kenizzites who lived in the Judean Negeb and the Arabah. The Kenites later settled in Harosheth-hagoiim (literally, workshop of the Gentiles) in the Galilee (Judges 4:2, 4:13, 4:16). The Hivites were apparently the woodcutters in Israel, having learned their trade in the forests of Lebanon from the Tyrians. The Hivites then worked the forests of Samaria—Hamor, their patriarch, having settled in Shechem. Eventually they settled in Gibeon where they adopted the Israelite religion and became the woodcutters of Israel (Joshua 9:27).

The assumption that the Hivites were the stonemasons who worked on the Temple derives from I Chronicles:

> And David commanded to gather together the strangers that were in the land of Israel; and he set masons to hew wrought stones to build the house of God.
>
> (I Chronicles 22:2)

Solomon followed suit:

> And Solomon numbered all the strangers that were in the land of Israel....And he set threescore and ten thousand of them to be bearers of burdens, and fourscore thousand to be hewers in the mountain.
>
> (II Chronicles 2:17–18)

Thereafter the artisans apparently organized themselves by families such as:

> ...the families of the house of them that wrought fine linen, of the house of Ashbea.
>
> (I Chronicles 4:21)

The metalworkers and the woodcutters were the most active on a daily basis. A man needed wood to build his house and furniture, his working tools and his weapons, chariots and boats. Wood was also needed for heating and metal smelting and stone houses and foundries used large quantities of wood and charcoal (Isaiah 54:16, 44:12). Wood was plentiful in the Sharon valley at Ramot-menashe and Shefar'am and in the mountains on either side of the Jordan.

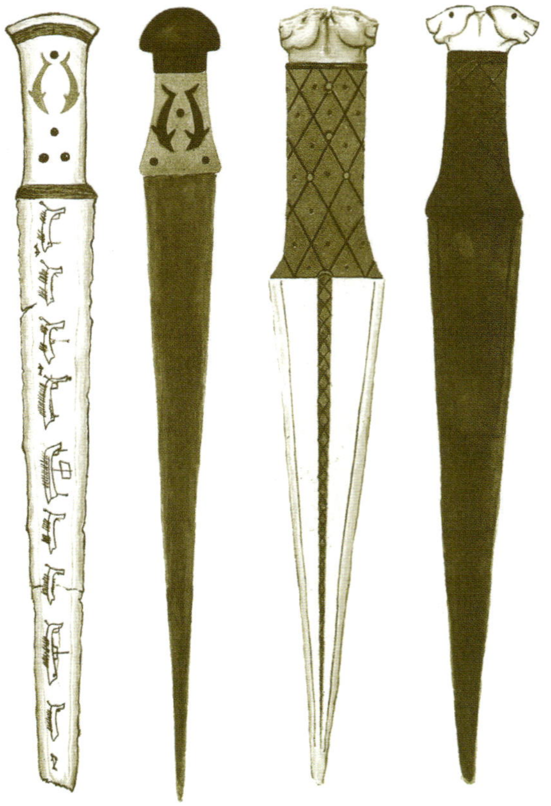

*Decorative daggers from Durak, near the Sea of Marmara* (courtesy M. Har-El).

The weapons industry was highly developed in Israel from the time of David and Solomon. The nation was always in a state of war preparedness and had to defend itself and improve the quality of its weapons. Professor Yigael Yadin in the Hebrew *Biblical Encyclopedia* writes that weapons were made for three purposes: for defense—the shield, helmet and armor; for attack—the hatchet, sword, lance, spear, bow and battering ram; and for transporting arms and warriors—the chariot.

Since hard and flexible wood grew in most parts of the country and iron was mined in Gilead, weapons were made in the northern part of the country. As the prophet Isaiah said:

> Behold, I have created the smith that bloweth the coals in the fire, and that bringeth forth an instrument for his work; and I have created the waster to destroy.
>
> (Isaiah 54:16)

Industry received a tremendous boost from Solomon's commercial ventures. He built a Mediterranean port at Tell Qasile near Joppa and the port he built at Ezion-geber on the Red Sea coast provided an outlet to the south and east. He gained control of the international overland routes—the Sea route, the King's Highway and the perfume route—and he developed seafaring with the aid of his Tyrian allies. Israel's international trade helped develop a number of its industries—woodworking, stonecutting, ironworks, the jewelry industry, pottery, weaving and dyeing, salt mining, the camphor industry, perfumes, wines and preserved foods such as olive oil.

Unlike the Canaanites who dwelled mainly in the plains, valleys and rifts, the Israelites' most intensive settlement, including the cities, was in the mountains on both sides of the river Jordan. The sources of wood, stone, and metal were primarily in the mountains (Deuteronomy 8:9; Joshua 17:18; Zechariah 6:1) and most of their industry was concentrated in the mountains and near cities.

Chronicles tells us about the stores of raw metals David built up in Jerusalem for constructing the Temple and building weapons:

> ...brass and iron without weight, for it is in abundance.
>
> (I Chronicles 22:14)

> ...and of brass eighteen thousand talents, and one hundred thousand talents of iron.
>
> (I Chronicles 29:7)

This amounts to 540 tons of bronze and 3,000 tons of iron.

II Kings 24 attests to the widespread activity of the smith and the craftsman in Jerusalem:

> And he carried away all Jerusalem, and all the princes, and all the mighty men of valour, even ten thousand captives, and all the craftsmen and smiths....And all the men of might, even seven thousand, and craftsmen and smiths a thousand, all that were strong and apt for war, even them the king of Babylon brought captive to Babylon.
>
> (II Kings 24:14, 16; see also Jeremiah 24:1, 29:2)

Thus a tenth of the exiles were smiths and craftsmen. This figure attests to the highly developed metal industry which existed in Jerusalem, a city situated in the midst of forests and relatively close to the iron mines of Gilead.

## SALT PITS

(Zephaniah 2:9)

The mine, or salt mine, is mentioned only once in the Bible. In Joshua "the city of Salt" (Joshua 15:62) is noted as being one of the six cities in the Judean Desert. How important was salt in the past, how was it produced during biblical and post-biblical times and how important was the salt mine?

Salt was one of the basic commodities. As Job states:

> Can that which is unsavoury be eaten without salt? or is there any taste in the white of an egg?
>
> (Job 6:6)

Leviticus notes the obligation to include salt in sacrifices:

> And every oblation of thy meat offering shalt thou season with salt; neither shalt thou suffer the salt of the covenant of thy God to be lacking from thy meat offering: with all thine offerings thou shalt offer salt.
>
> (Leviticus 2:13)

Ezekiel states that salt was used for cultic purposes:

> And thou shalt offer them before the LORD, and the priests shall cast salt upon them, and they shall offer them up for a burnt offering unto the LORD.
>
> (Ezekiel 43:24)

According to II Chronicles, salt symbolized the covenant between God and Israel:

# THE ECONOMY OF THE LAND OF ISRAEL

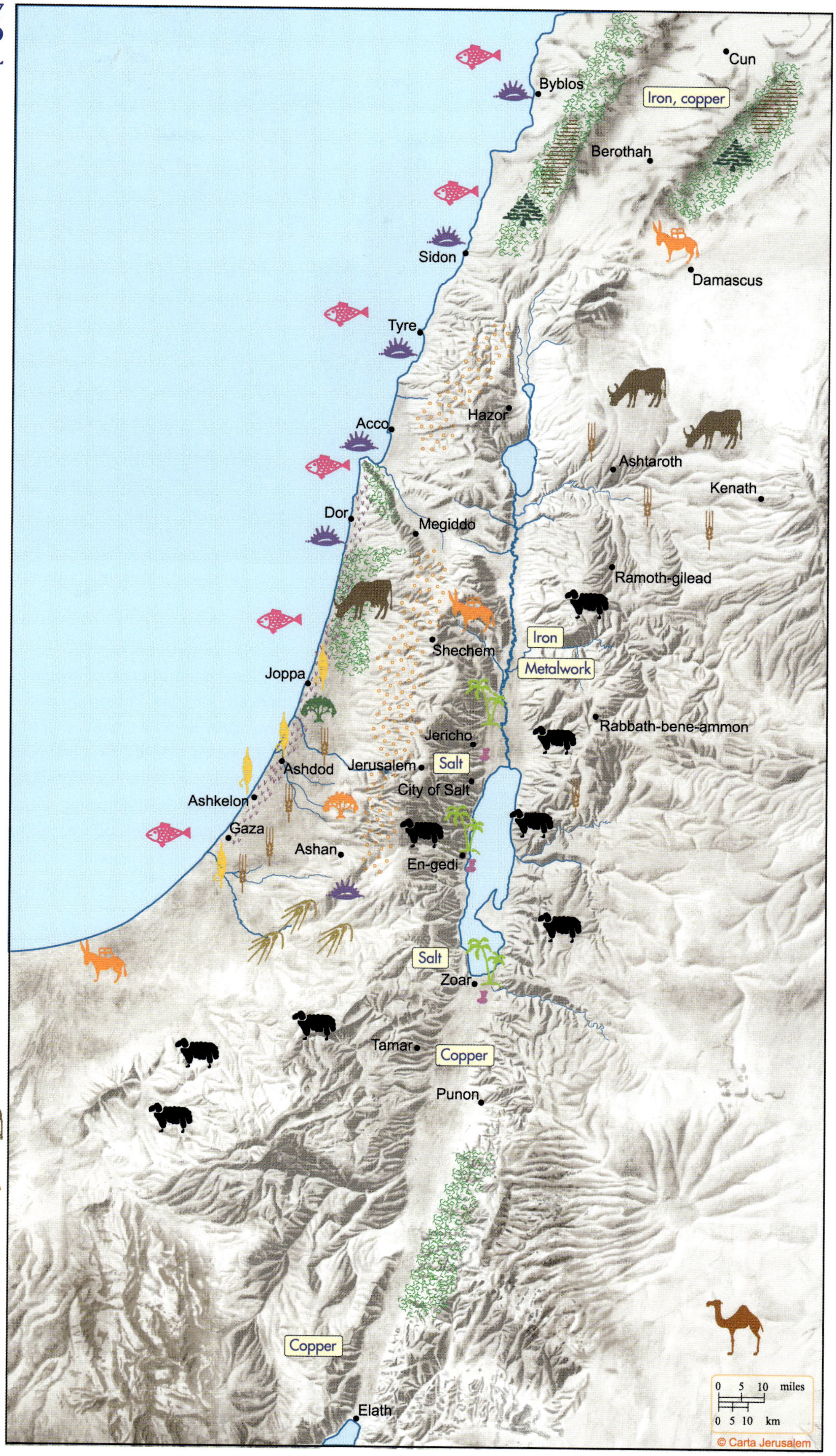


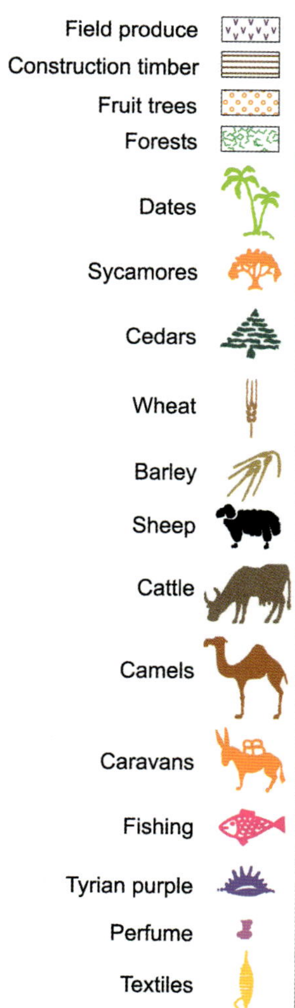

*Mount Sodom, showing the so-called "Lot's Wife" pillar* (photo Wilson44691 [public domain], via Wikimedia Commons).

the site or imply its close proximity to sources of salt.

Salt served many functions in biblical times. It was used as a condiment, in preserving fish, olives and vegetables, in the cheese and leather industries, and in medicine. A variety of salt compounds were used as digestifs, emetics, and in the treatment of intestinal worms and other parasitic afflictions. Salt was also used, in combination with honey and soda dates, in bandaging wounds. Salt was even used in separating metal from dross. Thus Ben-Sira (39:26) includes salt among man's most important necessities:

> Basic to all the needs of man's life are water and fire and iron and salt....

> Ought ye not to know that the LORD God of Israel gave the kingdom over Israel to David for ever, even to him and to his sons by a covenant of salt?
>
> (II Chronicles 13:5; see also Numbers 18:19)

These references to salt derive from its crucial importance to both man and beast. Blood, which symbolized the soul, contains salt:

> For the blood is the life....
>
> (Deuteronomy 12:23)

Blood also symbolized the covenant between God and Israel:

> And Moses took the blood, and sprinkled it on the people, and said, Behold the blood of the covenant, which the LORD hath made with you concerning all these words.
>
> (Exodus 24:8)

But salt, because it turns the otherwise fertile land of the Negeb, the Arabah and the Dead Sea plain into barren land (*meleha*=salt marsh), connotes desolation—a wasteland where sinners roam. Salt also destroys most cultivated crops:

> He turneth...a fruitful land into barrenness, for the wickedness of them that dwell therein.
>
> (Psalms 107:33–34)

> Whose house I have made the wilderness, and the barren land his dwellings.
>
> (Job 39:6)

> For he shall be like the heath in the desert, and shall not see when good cometh; but shall inhabit the parched places in the wilderness, in a salt land and not inhabited.
>
> (Jeremiah 17:6)

Desolate places, such as Ir-melah (City of Salt), Ge-melah (Valley of Salt), and Tel-melah (Hill of Salt), describe either the nature of

Now to the matter of where the salt was derived. Salt was derived from the Mediterranean Sea—as can be deduced from the Jerusalem Talmud's mention of Migdal-malha (Salt Tower; 22:1; 2; 3), in the vicinity of Atlit. Pliny notes that salt water was vaporized near Pelusium, contemporary Balluza, and near Memphis in Egypt. The Egyptian salt, however, was considered as being of inferior quality. The superior salt was neither that of the water of the Dead Sea, which when evaporated contained too much potassium, sulfur, etc., nor that of the Mediterranean Sea, but the salt mined from Mount Sodom.

Mount Sodom was not just the cheapest and most plentiful source of salt (it is still mined today) but it had some important advantages: strip mining, its year-round availability, and the fact that there was no need to wait for the seawater to evaporate before getting salt. The Mount Sodom saltstone has an excellent concentration of salt and it is pure. As to the salt's availability, Tosefta *Menahot* (9:15) tells us that the production of the superb Sodom salt never stops.

It is most probable that Zephaniah's reference is to the superior salt of Mount Sodom and to the salt of the Dead Sea, as most commentators have noted, because of its unhealthy composition. Thus Genesis states:

> And the vale of Siddim was full of slimepits....
>
> (Genesis 14:10)

meaning that the valley contained lime, gypsum and asphalt but not salt. Salt is mentioned in connection with Lot's wife:

> But his wife looked back from behind him, and she became a pillar of salt.
>
> (Genesis 19:26)

There are many pillars of salt at Mount Sodom.

# IR-HAMELAH (THE CITY OF SALT)

(Joshua 15:62)

Six Hebrew cities are mentioned in Joshua 15—Beth-arabah, Middin, Secacah, Nibshan, the City of Salt (Ir-hamelah) and En-gedi. But the only one designated by the term city is Ir-hamelah (*ir*=city). Let us examine the meaning of City of Salt before determining its location.

The designation City of Salt seems to point to a settlement where the inhabitants were engaged in the production of salt. This would seem to be a likely assumption because other towns in Israel were designated by their function—city of refuge for people who committed accidental manslaughter, city of fortifications for a walled city sealed by a double gate and a latch, royal city for the king's abode and holy city for a city with a temple. Thus it is probable that *the* City of Salt, with the emphasis on the definite article, suggests a city where the inhabitants were specifically engaged in the production and merchandising of salt.

It is well known that in ancient times, salt was a vital commodity used as a condiment in preserving fish and meat and in sacrifices as well as in the preparation of ritually edible meat. According to Mishnah *Middot* (5:3) there was a Salt Hall in the Temple which supplied the sacrificial salt, and according to Josephus (*Antiquities* 12.3.3) stores of salt were stocked in the Temple. Tosefta *Menahot* (9:15) notes that Sodom salt, mined from the inexhaustible and easily mined saltstone of Mount Sodom, was of superior quality.

Salt was so important to the suzerain ruler that from the time Israel came under Ptolemaic rule the salt industry became a royal monopoly. In fact a special tax was imposed on Israel's Jews obligating them to supply the court with a specified amount of salt on an annual basis. Where, then, was the City of Salt?

Y. Press, among others, assumed that Ir-hamelah was near Mount Sodom. M. Noth believes that Ir-hamelah was at Qumran (apparently Mezad-hasidim), on the northwest littoral of the Dead Sea either near Ein Feshkha or Enot Zuqim. His theory was strengthened by the findings of the Mezad-hasidim excavations which uncovered remnants of the Judean monarchy. Further evidence supporting Noth's contention was found after the Six-Day War when we were able to examine the site without interference. Dr. A. Davidi discovered a remarkable Roman road, parts of which were cut from the stone, others paved with stones and sections built on stone walls. The road emanates from the Dead Sea coast north of Mezad-hasidim, rises north of Wadi Mukheilih or Nahal Og or its vicinity, westward to Jerusalem. The road then continues past Nabi Musa, and the Khan el-Ahmar, which is near the Saint Euthymius Monastery, parallel to the Ma'aleh Adummim road.

One wonders why the ancients bothered paving an additional road near the Ma'aleh Adummim road, especially since the latter has less of an incline. The answer seems to be that the additional road was intended especially for transporting salt from Mount Sodom to Jerusalem and elsewhere. Our reasons for this assumption are as follows:

1. All along the route there are remnants of military outposts, army camps, water sources and a caravan inn which are from the Israelite, the Roman-Byzantine and the Arab periods.

2. The sixth-century Madaba map depicts two boats plying the Dead Sea laden with light and dark blocks of cargo. The light blocks would appear to be saltstone.

It is assumed that the ancients transported salt by sea from Mount Sodom to Ir-hamelah, presumably Mezad-hasidim, because sea transport was easier than overland shipment. From Mezad-hasidim the salt was trans-shipped on beasts of burden via Wadi Mukheilih to Jerusalem (Arabic *mukheilih* or *kalak* = boat). During stormy seas the boats made their way to Rujum el Bahr or Ma'aganit-hamelah (Hebrew *ma'aganit* = anchorage), a peninsula in the northern part of the Dead Sea. On an archaeological expedition in 1967 under Professor Yohanan Aharoni, we discovered that the anchorage measured 82 by 39 feet (25 by 12 m). From this protected anchorage salt was also transported via the salt route to Jerusalem. Thus Ir-hamelah (as stated, Mezad-hasidim) has a convenient anchorage which was Ma'aganit-hamelah on the Dead Sea's northern coast.

*Salt deposits by the Dead Sea* (photo Samuel Magal).

# NATURAL VEGETATION, TREES AND THEIR USES
# INTRODUCTION

*Ancient olive tree, City of David* (photo HolylandIsraelTours, via Wikimedia Commons).

According to Professor Y. Felix, there were about 2,300 different types of plants in the country in ancient times, about one hundred of which are mentioned in the Bible and about five hundred in the Mishnah and Talmud.

The relationship between man and flora in biblical times was profound, even so far as to compare man and fruit trees (Deuteronomy 20:19). Trees and bushes were essential. They provided shelter in summer; fuel for lighting, heating and cooking; charcoal for the metal industry where tools and weapons were manufactured, and for the glass and pottery industries; wood for furniture, buildings, chariots and wagons; fibers for rope, sacks and hats; raw materials for perfumes and medicines; and as the backdrop for courtship.

The Bible mentions three types of wood: *forest trees* (Isaiah 10:19; Ezekiel 15:6, 31:4–5; Song of Songs 2:3)—meaning wood of non-fruit-bearing trees; *trees of the field* (Isaiah 55:12; Ezekiel 17:24; Joel 1:12, 1:19)—fruit trees watered by precipitation; and *garden trees*, or irrigated orchards (Genesis 2:16, 3:2). The people were even required to plant fruit-bearing trees (Leviticus 19:23).

As to forest trees, our research shows that the Israelites were the first people mentioned in the Bible to plant non-fruit-bearing trees both in the mountain and desert regions. The following is brought as evidence of this activity:

1. The tree-planting pioneer was the Patriarch Abraham who planted a tamarisk tree (mentioned three times in the Bible) in the Negeb desert town of Beer-sheba: "Abraham planted a tamarisk tree in Beer-sheba, and called thereon the name of the Lord, the Everlasting God" (Genesis 21:33). Planting the tree was a sign of the covenant between the people of Israel and the Land of Israel because the tree is a sign of permanency and rootedness. Later, Saul, the first king of Israel, sat under a tamarisk in his capital of Gibeah, in the hills of Benjamin (I Samuel 22:6), despite the fact that the tamarisk's natural habitat is the desert valleys and the coastal sands. Saul might have done so for its symbolic value, in emulation of the first patriarch. Furthermore, Saul fell in battle against the Philistines on Mount Gilboa, and was buried "under a [tamarisk] tree at Jabesh" (I Samuel 31:13) in the Jordan Rift to the east of the Jordan River. Thus the tamarisk, a tall desert tree that thrives in salty sand and which has many leaves to provide shade for the weary

desert traveler, symbolized the attachment of the Israelites to the desolate regions of their country. The tamarisk is an evergreen and as such, belongs to a category of sanctified trees which includes the olive, cypress and oak (Deuteronomy 12:2; I Kings 14:23; Jeremiah 11:16; Hosea 14:8).

2. Ecclesiastes says of Solomon: "I made me pools of water, to water therewith the wood that bringeth forth trees" (Ecclesiastes 2:6). What kind of trees did Solomon plant and for what purpose? It appears that he planted the *oil tree*—pine, cypress and acacia which had to be planted in purity by Jews for decorating the Temple: "...he strengtheneth for himself among the trees of the forest: he planteth an ash, and the rain doth nourish it" (Isaiah 44:14). Solomon did indeed build doors, floors, lintels and cherubs for the Temple (I Kings 6:23, 6:31–33). Isaiah alludes to the planting of cypresses (Isaiah 55:13), whose wood was used for lining the floors and doors of the Temple and for making its musical instruments (I Kings 6:15, 6:34; II Samuel 6:5). The acacia, whose wood was used for building the Holy Ark, was watered by the Gihon Spring—"a fountain shall come forth of the house of the Lord, and shall water the valley of Shittim" (Joel 4:18)—Jerusalem's Nahal Kidron. It is likely that the frankincense, the fragrant spices and the dates of Solomon which were cultivated in the king's garden (II Kings 25:4; Jeremiah 39:4, 52:7) in the King's Valley (II Samuel 18:18) in Nahal Kidron, were watered by the King's Pool in the Gihon:

> And by the river upon the bank thereof, on this side and on that side, shall grow all trees for meat, whose leaf shall not fade, neither shall the fruit thereof be consumed: it shall bring forth new fruit according to his months, because their waters they issued out of the sanctuary: and the fruit thereof shall be for meat, and *the leaf thereof for medicine*.
>
> (Ezekiel 47:12; italics added)

Just as the eternal flame in the Tent of Meeting was fed continuously by olive oil (Exodus 27:20; Leviticus 24:2), the frankincense that burned there continuously (Exodus 30:8) was apparently grown in King Solomon's garden in Nahal Kidron.

## HOWL, FIR TREE; FOR THE CEDAR HAS FALLEN

(Zechariah 11:2)

This passage deals with two subjects: the lamentation on the destruction of the forest, and the wailing of the shepherds and the roaring of the lions:

> Open thy doors, O Lebanon, that the fire may devour thy cedars.
> Howl, fir tree; for the cedar is fallen; because the mighty are spoiled: howl, O ye oaks of Bashan; for the forest of the vintage is come down.
> There is a voice of the howling of the shepherds; for their glory is spoiled: a voice of the roaring of young lions; for the pride of Jordan is spoiled.
>
> (Zechariah 11:1–3)

The trees mentioned here are the fir, the cedar and the oak, which differ from each other by nature, habitat and use. The fir (or cypress) grew in Senir, which is Hermon, and in Lebanon. It is an upright, broad and very tall tree used for the construction of palaces and shrines. The fir was also used for flooring, as described in I Kings, in the construction of Solomon's Temple:

> ...and covered the floor of the house with planks of fir.
>
> (I Kings 6:15)

And in II Chronicles:

> And the greater house he cieled with fir tree.
>
> (II Chronicles 3:5)

The Temple doors were also made of fir or cypress wood, as stated in I Kings:

> And the two doors were of fir tree....
>
> (I Kings 6:34)

The cedar was the largest and thickest tree in the Middle East providing the best shade. Its habitat was in the Lebanese heights, and it was considered the tree of God because of its dimensions and great height:

> The hills were covered with the shadow of it, and the boughs thereof were like the goodly cedars.
>
> (Psalms 80:10)

And:

> The trees of the LORD are full of sap; the cedars of Lebanon, which he hath planted.
>
> (Psalms 104:16)

The two main uses of the cedar were for the construction of sanctuaries and shrines, as narrated of Solomon in I Kings 6:15:

> And he built the walls of the house within with boards of cedar, both the floor of the house and the walls of the cieling: and he covered them on the inside with wood....
>
> (I Kings 6:15)

And:

> He built also the house of the forest of Lebanon...upon four rows of cedar pillars, with cedar beams upon the pillars.
>
> (I Kings 7:2)

Cedars were also used for the construction of ships' masts by the Phoenicians, for the thicker and higher the mast, the larger the ship; and the fir was especially important for sailors as it was used to strengthen the larger vessels, as we find in Ezekiel:

> They have made all thy ship boards of fir trees of Senir: they have taken cedars from Lebanon to make masts for thee.
>
> (Ezekiel 27:5)

In the Song of Songs we find evidence of cedars used for furniture:

> The beams of our house are cedar, and our rafters of fir.
>
> (Song of Songs 1:17)

The oaks of Bashan, which according to scholars are the Tabor

*Cedars of Lebanon* (photo Snapshots of the Past, via Wikimedia Commons).

oaks, are wider and taller than the other species of oak, and its wood harder than that of all other forest trees. Thus they had numerous uses: the Phoenicians used them to make oars, as in Ezekiel:

> Of the oaks of Bashan have they made thine oars....
>
> (Ezekiel 27:6)

and the branches were manufactured into plows, tools and armaments and the planks of oak wood were turned into threshing sledges.

We believe that pastureland and forests are interconnected, for in the forest there is both shade and fresh grass. Thus the hill country is described in the Bible as an ideal sheep-rearing zone, as in Ezekiel:

> My sheep wandered through all the mountains, and upon every high hill.
>
> (Ezekiel 34:6)

The prophet Micah also mentions sheep-rearing in the Bashan, the Carmel, and in Gilead:

> Feed thy people with thy rod, the flock of thine heritage, which dwell solitarily in the wood, in the midst of Carmel: let them feed in Bashan and Gilead, as in the days of old.
>
> (Micah 7:14)

With the destruction of the forest the pastures were also lost, as the shepherds wail:

> There is a voice of the howling of the shepherds; for their glory is spoiled....
>
> (Zechariah 11:3)

Control over the mountain peaks and their forests was very important in ancient times, for the shrines were built on the peaks and the value of the forest trees was very great. Hence the destruction of the forest is a symbol of the days of the Lord's judgment when war will break out: the high places will be lowered and the lofty cut down, as stated in Isaiah:

> For the day of the LORD of hosts shall be upon every one that is proud and lofty, and upon every one that is lifted up; and he shall be brought low:
>
> And upon all the cedars of Lebanon, that are high and lifted up, and upon all the oaks of Bashan.
>
> (Isaiah 2:12–13)

Similar references are found in chapter 10:

> Behold, the Lord, the LORD of hosts, shall lop the bough with terror: and the high ones of stature shall be hewn down, and the haughty shall be humbled.
>
> And he shall cut down the thickets of the forest with iron, and Lebanon shall fall by a mighty one.
>
> (Isaiah 10:33–34)

Isaiah also prophesies in the same vein about the rise of Sennacherib:

> By thy servants hast thou reproached the Lord, and hast said, By the multitude of my chariots am I come up to the height of the mountains, to the sides of Lebanon; and I will cut down the tall cedars thereof, and the choice fir trees thereof: and I will enter into the height of his border, and the forest of his Carmel.
>
> (Isaiah 37:24)

When the Chaldeans are defeated, however, and in the time of peace and tranquility, the trees of the forest will grow once again without fear, as the prophet declares:

> The whole earth is at rest, and is quiet: they break forth into singing.
>
> Yea, the fir trees rejoice at thee, and the cedars of Lebanon, saying, Since thou art laid down, no feller is come up against us.
>
> (Isaiah 14:7–8)

The phrase "the forest of the vintage" (*ya'ar habazir*) in the opening quotation is problematic. The written form of the Hebrew is *bazur* (fortified), while it is read as *bazir* (vintage). Some views hold that the forest served as a fortified wall against the enemy, with the function of a fortified city. There would, however, appear to be two other explanations: the first is that most forests lay in the mountains which served as natural defenses, hence the term "fortified forest," and the second explains the verse:

> ...howl, O ye oaks of Bashan; for the forest of the vintage is come down.
>
> (Zechariah 11:2)

The mountains of the Bashan may be identified with the present-day Mount of the Druze, where vines were cultivated in the past—the high-quality wine of Hauran is mentioned in tractate *Keritot* 6 as "old white wine."

Thus with the destruction of the forest the enemy also wiped out the vines, and following this the vintage. It is worth noting that the forests in this chapter of Zechariah are mentioned in descending order of altitude of growth: the snow-covered peaks of the Hermon is the habitat of the fir or cypress, which, according to Prof. Zohari, tolerates temperatures of up to 52 degrees below zero; below are the cedars, and their howl is heard with the tree-feller; and the oaks grow on the lower slopes of the mountains of Bashan, and with their destruction we hear the wailing of the shepherds, because of the loss of their livelihood. Lower still, in the depths of the Jordan Valley and along its banks, we find the tamarisk and willow, and this was the home of the lions whose roar is heard when their place of shelter is cut down.

## FOR THE JUNGLE OF [THE] JORDAN IS SPOILED

(Zechariah 11:3)

This passage from the prophet mentions the forests of Lebanon and the jungle of the Jordan. Before examining the connection between these two very different regions, we will describe the landscape of the Jordan Valley and its jungle vegetation area, and ascertain their influence on human activity and the behavior of the domestic and wild animals living there.

The middle and lower Jordan Valley is 65 miles (105 km) in length, while its width varies from 6 miles (10 km) in the north, 2.5 to 3 miles (4 to 5 km) in the center and over 12 miles (20 km) in the south. In the north of the Jordan Valley the river lies at 656 feet (200 m) below the level of the Mediterranean Sea, while in the south it reaches 1,312 feet (400 m) below. Running across the valley from the jungle to the mountains on either side of the river, there are three sections, each with an escarpment which acts as a barrier to passage. The first is the floodplain of the Jordan, which includes the rich vegetation of the jungle and is approximately 0.6 mile (1 km) wide. Beyond the floodplain the landscape is hilly and the height of the hill scarp descending to the floodplain is 130 to 200 feet (40 to 60 m). When this scarp built of Lissan marl is wet, it constitutes a muddy barrier to the passage of man and beast.

The second section is the Jordan Valley which is 2 to 4 miles (3 to 6 km) wide on either side of the river; it is generally flat with a slope descending approximately 33 to 50 feet (10 to 15 m) to the hills, but there are also small intermediate scarps within it. The third section consists of the mountain scarps on either side of the Jordan, reaching an altitude of 3,937 feet (1,200 m) in Gilead, and 2,950 to 3,280 feet (900 to 1,000 m) above sea level in Samaria and Judah. The high mountain escarpments result in the appearance of yet another barrier, which is climatic in nature: the summer winds descending from the mountains of Gilead, Samaria and Judah to the Jordan Valley, 4,590 to 5,250 feet (1,400 to 1,600 m) below, heat and dry the air to such an extent that living conditions are hard for both man and beast. The high summer temperatures and low relative humidity in the valley result in the evaporation of 6.5 to 8 feet (2 to 2.5 m) of water per annum and the consequent salination of the soil.

Conditions are particularly difficult in the jungle where the thick tree growth prevents the passage of fresh air. The steep mountains are the origin of numerous gorges and river tributaries which carry the floodwaters and the rivers down to the Jordan Valley. These rivers cut ravines in the Lissan marl, which results in the formation of waterfalls and steep valley walls in the marl, all of which constitute barriers to passage. On the other hand, the large quantity of silt carried down to the Jordan by its tributaries builds fording points along the valley, thus facilitating passage from one bank to the other.

From this description we learn that the jungle of the Jordan is not conducive to animal or human life. The Jordan floodplain, which is the habitat of the forests and wild animals, is flooded in winter and spring; the soils of the hills on the side of the floodplain are composed of gypsum marls and their salinity renders them bare of vegetation; and the unbearable summer climate—all form the antithesis of human settlement. The wild animals and cattle, on the other hand, find shelter in the thick forest of the Jordan floodplain, and the numerous fording points enable the passage of man and beast and maintain contact between the two populated banks of the river. Hence the Jordan constitutes both a lifeline and a barrier,

*Bathing-place on the Jordan, 19th century engraving* (Carta collection).

with the fords constituting the link in the chain.

The first three verses of our chapter in Zechariah describe the various forest regions:

> Open thy doors, O Lebanon, that the fire may devour thy cedars.
> Howl, fir tree; for the cedar is fallen; because the mighty are spoiled: howl, O ye oaks of Bashan; for the forest of the vintage is come down.
> There is a voice of the howling of the shepherds; for their glory is spoiled: a voice of the roaring of young lions; for the jungle of the Jordan is spoiled.
>
> (Zechariah 11:1–3)

The different geographical landscapes of the forests are described: the fir and cedar grow in the mountains of Lebanon, the highest mountains in the Land of Israel; the oak grows on the Bashan heights, which is of medium altitude, while no species of tree is mentioned in the jungle of the Jordan, which is the lowest region of all. The reason why the trees growing in this last area are not given specific mention may be that the willow, the tamarisk and the poplar, which grow in the Jordan Valley, have no industrial or commercial value as do the cedar, the fir and the oak, without which human economic activity would be greatly lacking. The difference between the forests of Lebanon and Bashan, and that of the jungle of the Jordan lies in the fact that the felling of the trees in the latter brings ruin to the shepherds and livestock, as well as disaster for the lions and other forest animals. Although wild animals and livestock wandered in the forests of Lebanon and Bashan, they would not suffer so greatly if the forest was cut down, since it renews itself naturally. The jungle forest, on the other hand, would not be renewed in this way. It served as an important bridge for the livestock and wild animals of the forests as they wandered from one side of the Jordan to the other. For this reason the prophet emphasizes the cries and anxiety of both shepherds and lions:

> There is a voice of the howling of the shepherds; for their glory is spoiled: a voice of the roaring of young lions; for the jungle of the Jordan is spoiled.
>
> (Zechariah 11:3)

# WE HANGED OUR HARPS UPON THE WILLOWS

(Psalms 137:2)

Before discussing the habitat of the willows and their characteristics, it is essential to clarify the meaning of the word *arabah*, its geographical location and its uses. The Arabic word *arav*, according to the Al-Munjid dictionary, means abundant, clear water, or a river with a strong flow, i.e., a perennial stream. Another connotation of the word is a desert dweller, or a nomadic Bedouin who wanders from place to place, since in the desert there are springs of water and wells in the wadis and these were the only transportation routes. We read of water flowing in desert streams in Isaiah:

> ...for in the wilderness shall waters break out, and streams in the desert [*arabah*].
>
> (Isaiah 35:6)

And:

> ...he will make her wilderness like Eden, and her desert [*arabah*] like the garden of the Lord.
>
> (Isaiah 51:3)

Ezekiel prophesies:

> Then said he unto me, These waters issue out toward the east country, and go down into the desert [*arabah*], and go into the sea: which being brought forth into the sea, the waters shall be healed.
>
> (Ezekiel 47:8)

The geographical region of the Arabah is one of the most important longitudinal zones of the country, extending from the Sea of Galilee to the Gulf of Elath. It may be divided into three subregions: first, the Jordan Valley from the Sea of Galilee to the Dead Sea, which is the zone of the permanent flow of the Jordan and its tributaries on either side, and the habitat of the willow (*arabah*); the playas were used for the irrigated cultivation of dates, and the silts were used for growing cereals and flax. The second zone is the Dead Sea, which is termed the Sea of the Plain (*arabah*) in Deuteronomy (Deuteronomy 3:17, 4:49) and elsewhere; the numerous playas and erosion fans of the rivers were used for the cultivation of dates and persimmon, and other spices in areas that were not saline. Permanent settlements in both these regions were founded near the springs that flowed at the foot of the mountains. The third region was the Arabah desert or plain, which extended from the Dead Sea in the north to the Gulf of Elath in the south (Deuteronomy 1:1; Jeremiah 50:12, 51:43). It was characterized by its function as an area of transit, and its oases served the trading caravans that brought imported goods from the Gulf of Elath and the copper and iron ores of the Arabah. As in other desert areas, here, too, goat and camel herdsmen wandered with their livestock, and some of these nomads would rob the commercial caravans.

Another meaning of the term *arabah* in the Bible is a valley or ravine between mountains, as we find in Joshua 8:14:

> And it came to pass, when the king of Ai saw it, that they hasted and rose up early, and the men of the city went out against Israel to battle, he and all his people, at a time appointed, before the... [*arabah*]; but he wist not that there were liers in ambush against him behind the city.
>
> (Joshua 8:14)

*"They that carried us away captive required of us a song"* (Psalms 137:3). *Alabaster relief from palace of Sennacherib (705–681 BCE)* (courtesy of the Trustees of the British Museum).

Or in II Kings:

And the city was broken up, and all the men of war fled by night by the way of the gate between two walls, which is by the king's garden: (now the Chaldees were against the city round about:) and the king went the way toward the...[*arabah*].

(II Kings 25:4)

Another reference is found in Deuteronomy:

Are they not on the other side Jordan, by the way where the sun goeth down, in the land of the Canaanites, which dwell in the ... [*arabah*] over against Gilgal, beside the plains of Moreh?

(Deuteronomy 11:30)

In view of these biblical references, it emerges that the Arabah is not only the longitudinal arid valley of the Land of Israel, but can indicate low areas between mountains to the east of the main valley, into which most of the rivers drain. The willow plant (*arava*), then, grows in desert regions near running water, which is the linkage of its name to rivers and their tributaries, as in Job:

The shady trees cover him with their shadow; the willows of the brook compass him about.

(Job 40:22)

And in Isaiah:

Therefore the abundance they have gotten, and that which they have laid up, shall they carry away to the brook of the willows.

(Isaiah 15:7)

The willow of the brook is one of the four species taken by the Israelites for worship during the Feast of Tabernacles, as in Leviticus:

And ye shall take you on the first day the boughs of goodly [citron] trees, branches of palm trees, and the boughs of thick trees, and willows of the brook; and ye shall rejoice before the LORD your God seven days.

(Leviticus 23:40)

According to Professor M. Zohari, the rapid growth of the willow symbolizes the prosperity and vigor of the people of Israel, as the prophet Isaiah expresses:

And they shall spring up as among the grass, as willows by the water courses.

(Isaiah 44:4)

The willows of the rivers of Babylon mentioned in our chapter, which are the willows along the river Euphrates, symbolize the mourning, lamentation and yearning for Zion, where the mourners refused to sing holy songs on foreign soil, as emphasized in Psalm 137:

By the rivers of Babylon, there we sat down, yea, we wept, when we remembered Zion.
We hanged our harps upon the willows in the midst thereof.
For there they that carried us away captive required of us a song; and they that wasted us required of us mirth, saying, Sing us one of the songs of Zion.
How shall we sing the LORD'S song in a strange land?

(Psalms 137:1–4)

Professor Zohari explains that throughout Babylon, the willow is a cultivated, decorative tree with long, drooping branches. The exiles from Israel, on seeing the drooping leaves of the willow trailing in the water, might well have been moved to tears. It is also a fact that the popular name of this tree is the weeping willow. The willow also grows in Israel along the perennial streams. The willow brought to Jerusalem on the Feast of Tabernacles came from Mozah to the west of the city, as explained in the Mishnah, *Succah* 4:5:

What was the rite of the willow-branch? There was a place below Jerusalem called Mozah. They went down and collected young willow-branches, and they came and set them upright along the sides of the Altar.

The plucking of willow branches at Mozah proves that during the time of the Mishnah water flowed in the stream that originated in the marl stream at Mozah.

## LET US GO, WE PRAY THEE, UNTO JORDAN, AND TAKE THENCE EVERY MAN A BEAM, AND LET US MAKE US A PLACE THERE, WHERE WE MAY DWELL

(II Kings 6:2)

This chapter narrates how the disciples of the prophets were looking for living quarters, and on turning to Elisha, the suggestion was accepted. We will first explain why the disciples went to the Jordan to cut logs, what sort of living quarters they built from only one log, and then we will discuss other types of structures that were made out of wood from the forest.

The forests of the Land of Israel grew in three large geographical regions: on the rainy mountains which were the home of the common oak and the terebinth (*Pistacia palaestina*); in the Sharon region where the Tabor oak was found; and in the jungle of the Jordan. The latter is the lowest and hottest part of the Jordan Valley, where the ebb and flow of the Jordan saturate the earth at frequent intervals. Hence the banks of the Jordan were covered with the thickest forest of the whole country. This dense vegetation was the home of many wild animals in ancient times. According to Professor M. Zohari, the vegetation of the jungle grows in separate bands of species which extend from the river itself to the banks and beyond. The water is the home of the cane and the reed, and the winter- and spring-flooded area is the habitat of the poplar, the tamarisk and the willow. All these species, which grow in large amounts of water and on saline soil, are too weak and fragile to be used in the manufacture of permanent structures, for they cannot withstand the forces of nature over long periods. Their advantages lie in their rapid growth and their thick, shady branches. Thus the ancients used them to build huts, particularly in the arid and semiarid regions which do not receive much rainfall in the winter, and are subject to the extreme summer heat.

How did the disciples of the prophets manage with only one log

*The Jordan Valley* (courtesy M. Har-El).

for their hut? It would appear that the hut was circular in shape, and was built of one log which was stuck into the ground in the center of the circle. At a radius of 10 to 13 feet (3 to 4 m) around it, the builders dug a circular channel, fixing the wide end of the branches into the ground, while the other end was tied to the vertical log in the middle. A narrow opening was left on the north side, which was sheltered from the sun, in the same way that the Indians do today. A hint of this practice is found in Job:

> He buildeth his house as a moth [*'ash*], and as a booth that the keeper maketh.
>
> (Job 27:18)

The word *'ash* in Hebrew means a bird's nest and the "booth" is explained by Saadiah Gaon as a branch of nests, taken from the jungle of the Jordan. Hence there is some correlation between the round bird's nest and the watchman's hut.

Why did the disciples of the prophet move their living quarters and where did they settle? The first verse of our chapter (II Kings 6:1) offers an explanation:

> And the sons of the prophets said unto Elisha, Behold now, the place where we dwell with thee is too strait for us.

It seems that Elisha's home of Abel-meholah in the southern Beth-shean Valley was, in fact, overcrowded, since all the agricultural land was cultivated. Thus, the disciples had to move to the Jordan jungle where there were flooded agricultural islands during the winter that could be cultivated by the farmers. This was probably an area of "no-man's land" because of the wild animals, and the river floods which often washed away both the soil and the human and animal inhabitants. The verse quoted tells us of the residences of the disciples:

> ...and let us make us a place there, where we may dwell.
>
> (II Kings 6:2)

The hut, or booth, was built as a temporary place of residence in many parts of the country, and had several functions. It gave protection from the sun, serving the shepherds who roamed the wilderness, as in Leviticus:

> That your generations may know that I made the children of Israel to dwell in booths, when I brought them out of the land of Egypt....
>
> (Leviticus 23:43)

We also find evidence in Genesis where the Bible tells of Jacob and his cattle:

> And Jacob journeyed to Succoth, and built him an house, and made booths for his cattle: therefore the name of the place is called Succoth.
>
> (Genesis 33:17)

Jacob apparently arrived at Succoth on the banks of the Jabbok in the Jordan Valley during the spring, for he says to Esau:

> My lord knoweth that the children are tender, and the flocks and herds with young are with me: and if men should overdrive them one day, all the flock will die.
>
> (Genesis 33:13)

We learn here that the animals were nursing, and since the sheep usually have their lambs during the winter, Jacob must have reached Succoth at the end of the winter. In the spring there is fresh pastureland for a period of two months in the Jordan Valley. The booths built by Jacob for his flock were probably made in the shape of a triangle, with the logs set up in the middle, and the branches laid on the two walls like a hut, whereas the house he built was made of clay and mud similar to those of the Bedouin in the Jordan Valley today.

Another booth that gave protection from the burning sun is found in Jonah 4:5:

> So Jonah went out of the city, and sat on the east side of the city, and there made him a booth, and sat under it in the shadow.
>
> (Jonah 4:5)

And in Isaiah 4:6:

> And there shall be a tabernacle for a shadow in the daytime from the heat.
>
> (Isaiah 4:6)

The booth was also used as a hiding place, as we find in Psalm 27:

> For in the time of trouble he shall hide me in his pavilion [*succah*]:
> in the secret of his tabernacle he shall hide me....
>
> (Psalms 27:5)

Another function was a place of ambush for wild animals, as in Psalm 10:

> He lieth in wait secretly as a lion in his den:
> he lieth in wait to catch the poor....
>
> (Psalms 10:9)

or in Job:

> When they couch in their dens, and abide in the covert to lie in wait?
>
> (Job 38:40)

The booth was also used by farmers in the vineyard to store the fruit during the vintage season, as expressed by Isaiah:

> And the daughter of Zion is left as a cottage in a vineyard,
> as a lodge in a garden of cucumbers....
>
> (Isaiah 1:8)

Sometimes the booth was built on top of a tower, as in Isaiah:

> ...and built a tower in the midst of it....
>
> (Isaiah 5:2)

in order to give protection from dangerous animals and reptiles, as well as from thieves. Finally, the *succah* was used by soldiers in military camps, as narrated in I Kings 20:12, in the siege of Samaria by Ben-hadad:

> ...as he was drinking, he and the kings in the pavilions [*succoth*].....
>
> (I Kings 20:12)

and in the siege of Rabbath-ammon, narrated in II Samuel 11:11:

> And Uriah said unto David, The ark, and Israel, and Judah, abide in tents [*succoth*]; and my lord Joab, and the servants of my lord, are encamped in the open fields; shall I then go into mine house, to eat and to drink, and to lie with my wife?
>
> (II Samuel 11:11)

# THEN DAVID DEPARTED, AND CAME INTO THE FOREST [*YA'AR*] OF HARETH

(I Samuel 22:5)

The full quotation of this verse runs as follows:

> And the prophet Gad said unto David, Abide not in the hold; depart, and get thee into the land of Judah. Then David departed, and came into the forest [*ya'ar*] of Hareth.
>
> (I Samuel 22:5)

The question of the location of the forest of Hareth has puzzled the scholars, and their opinions on the matter are divided. Most of them feel that the forest mentioned in this passage is a wooded area in the Shephelah (lowland), and Judean Hills or the Judean Desert. What is puzzling here is what David and his followers were doing in the Shephelah and the hills, and how could a forest have grown in the wilderness of Ziph and Maon, which were the areas of David's wanderings in the Judean Desert? It seems inconceivable that there should be a forest in the desert. Since the forest of Hareth is mentioned only once in the Bible one cannot rely solely on the scriptural text and the etymological significance of the name must be sought, as well as reference to the geographical and topographical structure of the wilderness of Ziph and Maon.

The meaning of the word *ya'ar*, or *wa'ar* in Arabic, is a fearsome, rocky or hilly area, lacking dense vegetation. The Hebrew root is *aro* (*'rh*), meaning exposed or bare, like Maareh-geba in the Bible. In biblical Hebrew the word *ya'ar* has a double meaning: generally it refers to a wooded area, but sometimes indicates a desolate zone difficult to cultivate. Isaiah exclaims:

> The burden upon Arabia. In the forest [*ya'ar*], in Arabia shall ye lodge, O ye travelling companies of Dedanim.
>
> (Isaiah 21:13)

It is highly improbable that a forest could grow in the wilderness of Arabia (*'arab*). A more likely hypothesis is that the Semite nomads of the wastes of Arabia termed their settlements *ya'ar*, in the Arabic sense of a wasteland (*ya'ar–wa'ar*), and when they began to settle the cultivated regions of the Mediterranean, the meaning of the term *ya'ar* was transferred to the wooded forest, which also did not yield fruit and which was located chiefly in the rocky hills suitable only for sheep grazing.

*A desert canyon* (photo Samuel Magal).

Evidence of this interpretation is in Micah's prophecy:

> Therefore shall Zion for your sake be plowed as a field, and Jerusalem shall become heaps, and the mountain of the house as the high places of the forest [*ya'ar*].
>
> (Micah 3:12)

This passage is a clear description of the destruction of the city, for after the enemy had conquered it they would plow it over, turning it into mounds of rubble and wasteland. Similar imagery is found in Hosea 2:12:

> And I will destroy her vines and her fig trees, whereof she hath said, These are my rewards that my lovers have given me: and I will make them a forest [*ya'ar*], and the beasts of the field shall eat them.
>
> (Hosea 2:12)

Here, too, there is correlation between "I will *destroy* her vines and her fig trees" and "I will make them a forest," both referring to the fertile turning into waste. Hence "beasts of the field shall eat them," meaning that the land would become pasture.

As to the geographic location of this forest, we may learn something from the adjective in the name "forest of *Hareth*." The word *hareth* means engraved, or indented, so that the location of the forest of Hareth should be sought in that part of the Judean Desert which, on the one hand, is rocky and used for pasturing and, on the other, is indented by numerous ravines. Since David and his men took care of the flocks of Nabal the Carmelite, and also engaged in robbery, the forest of Hareth must lie in a grazing area on a major transportation junction in the desert, where taxes could be collected from the travelers, or the livestock caravans robbed. The forest of Hareth could be identified with the Valley of Qannaim to the west of Masada; this valley is deeply indented by numerous ravines and it is also the location of an important junction. The main lateral route from Hebron via the Zeelim Valley passed this way to Masada and Moab, and its course had abundant water resources. It is probable that David led his parents to Moab this way when he fled from Saul, using the same route back to the forest of Hareth on the instructions of the prophet Gad. It was here that Saul encamped in his pursuit of David, as mentioned in I Samuel:

> And Saul pitched in the hill of Hachilah, which is before Jeshimon [i.e., the wilderness], by the way. But David abode in the wilderness....
>
> (I Samuel 26:3)

This route was also used to bring the large flocks of Moab, the cradle of sheep farming, to the kingdom of Judah.

There is one longitudinal route in the Judean Desert which follows a syncline running along the whole length of the desert: from the Qannaim Valley in the south, where it crosses the Zeelim Valley, as far as the vale of Hyrcania near Jericho in the north, at the crossing point of the Kidron Valley. Thus it seems likely that the Qannaim Valley is the biblical *ya'ar* of Hareth; this is apparently the "Arabah" mentioned in connection with David and his followers in I Samuel:

> ...David and his men were in the wilderness of Maon, in the plain on the south of Jeshimon.
>
> (I Samuel 23:24)

At this important junction David could well have supported four hundred to five hundred men by robbery and plunder, by collecting taxes from the shepherds for protection, and by exacting toll payments from the caravans passing here. He would also have been able to control the eastern entry to the Hebron Hills, on the way to the wilderness of Ziph and Maon.

## THOU SHALT OBSERVE THE FEAST OF TABERNACLES [*SUCCOTH*] SEVEN DAYS

(Deuteronomy 16:13)

The precept of building the *succah* (booth) involved the use of the leaves of the olive tree, the wild olive, the myrtle, the palm and the thick tree. There were three extensive geographical regions in the Land of Israel where forests were prevalent. The first was the rainy mountainous zone, which was characterized by the common oak, the "oil tree," which according to Professor Y. Felix is the Jerusalem pine, the olive, which grew on the Mount of Olives and in hidden niches in the hills, and the myrtle—all of them evergreen. The second forest zone was in the Sharon plain which was the home of the Tabor oak, the most common tree in the country, with numerous uses in industry, and the citron tree, whose fruit, the ethrog, was used in the ritual of the feast of Succoth. The third region was the jungle of the Jordan, where the chief species were the willow which embellished the forest, and the palms which were cultivated at the oases and were used for the lulab (palm branch) required in the Succoth ritual.

### The Uses of the *Succah* (Booth)

The *succah* was constructed from trees and bushes whose branches were joined together to form a protective roof against the heat of the sun. Its uses during the biblical period were numerous, but its function was always that of a temporary structure. The booths were the homes of the *desert nomads*, as in Leviticus:

> I made the children of Israel to dwell in booths, when I brought them out of the land of Egypt.
>
> (Leviticus 23:43)

They served as *shelters for livestock* in the pastures, as we find in the narrative of Jacob who journeyed to Succoth in Genesis:

> ...and built him an house, and made booths for his cattle.
>
> (Genesis 33:17)

They were also used as *living quarters for soldiers in the battlefield*, as Uriah the Hittite explains to David during the siege of Rabbath-ammon in II Samuel 11:11:

> The ark, and Israel, and Judah, abide in tents [*succoth*]; and my lord Joab, and the servants of my lord, are encamped in the open fields....
>
> (II Samuel 11:11)

and in the siege of Samaria by King Ben-hadad of Aram in I Kings (I Kgs 20:12, 20:16). The booths were also the *lairs of wild animals* in the forest, as in Psalm 10:

He lieth in wait secretly as a lion in his den [*succah*]....

(Psalms 10:9)

or in Job:

Wilt thou hunt the prey for the lion? or fill the appetite of the young lions,
When they crouch in their dens, and abide in the covert [*succah*] to lie in wait?

(Job 38:39–40)

Finally, they were used by man, as is narrated of Jonah:

...and sat on the east side of the city, and there made him a booth [*succah*], and sat under it in the shadow....

(Jonah 4:5)

while the most important use of the *succah* was during the Feast of Tabernacles, or *Succoth*, when the Israelites dwelt in it for seven days. This festival is one of the three important agricultural feasts of the Jewish people.

The Feast of Tabernacles was so important to the people that it continued to be joyfully celebrated throughout the Second Temple period, and later on, even in underground conditions. The Book of Maccabees (10:6) relates that when the Hasmoneans purified the Temple on the Feast of Chanukah:

They celebrated the eight days in joy as on the Festival of Tabernacles, remembering the evil times when the Festival of Tabernacles had been celebrated in the *mountains and caves*, as though they were wild animals.

The festival is also mentioned in the time of the King Alexander Yannai, when the people pelted him with citrons (ethrogs) in the Temple (Josephus, *Antiquities* 13.13.5).

### The Special Characteristics of the Feast of Succoth

This festival has three different names which define the nature of the feast: Succoth, the Feast of the Ingathering and the Festival of the Lord.

*Succoth*: this name is connected to the acacia tree from which the Israelites built the Ark of the Covenant, the Tabernacle and the altar in the wilderness (Exodus 25:10, 26:15, 27:1; Deuteronomy 10:3). The first *succah* was probably built by the Israelites during their wanderings in the wilderness, from the branches of the acacia. This tree, which is also called lotus, grows in the desert wadis where the floodwaters provide moisture for the tree. The acacia is the most important tree in the desert since it provides man with shade from the sun and affords protection for both man and beast. The prophet Isaiah declares:

And there shall be a tabernacle [*succah*] for a shadow in the daytime from the heat, and for a place of refuge, and for a covert from storm and from rain.

(Isaiah 4:6)

Here the reference is probably to the acacia or lotus, for Job also describes the shady trees (hence its Hebrew name *ze'ela=zel*, meaning shade) in the river course, where man may find shelter:

*Booths on the housetops at Banias (Caesarea Philippi), 19th century engraving* (Carta collection).

He lieth under the shady trees, in the covert of the reed, and fens.
The shady trees cover him with their shadow;
the willows of the brook compass him about.

(Job 40:21–22)

The "storm and rain" mentioned by Isaiah is significant. Two features of the desert wadis give protection from the rain, particularly during the dangerous winter floods: the acacia provides the wanderer with shelter from the rain and he can climb onto it for safety during the floods; and secondly, the high rocks along the valley and on its banks, which provide man with shelter, is described in Job 24:8:

They are wet with the showers of the mountains,
and embrace the rock for want of a shelter.

(Job 24:8)

When the Israelites began building permanent settlements, they used the trees of the forest to build the *succah*:

And that they should publish and proclaim in all their cities, and in Jerusalem, saying, Go forth unto the mount, and fetch olive branches, and pine branches, and myrtle branches, and palm branches, and branches of thick trees, to make booths, as it is written.

(Nehemiah 8:15)

The festival is also known as the *Feast of the Ingathering* since it is celebrated in the autumn at the end of the agricultural year, when the farmer gathers in all his crops to the threshing floor and wine press (Deuteronomy 16:13). His crops included the olive and the vine, the date palm and grains, all of which were stored for the winter. The festival was celebrated in remembrance of the wanderings of the Israelites in the wilderness when they dwelt in booths, in order to renew the covenant with the Lord as commanded by Moses (Deuteronomy 31:9–11; II Chronicles 8:13), since the fertility of the soil depended on the rains which were a gift from Heaven.

The name *Festival of the Lord* is mentioned in Leviticus:

Also in the fifteenth day of the seventh month…ye shall keep a feast unto the LORD seven days.

(Leviticus 23:39)

The Lord's feast is a tradition of the agricultural festival when the people made their pilgrimage to worship God, and dates back as early as the time of the Judges when pilgrimages were made to Shiloh:

Then they said, Behold, there is a feast of the LORD in Shiloh yearly.

(Judges 21:19)

Elkanah, the father of Samuel the prophet, also made the pilgrimage to Shiloh:

And the man Elkanah, and all his house, went up to offer unto the LORD the yearly sacrifice, and his vow.

(I Samuel 1:21)

This festival had special significance because of its being *the* festival, when Solomon assembled all the communities of Israel on the completion of the Temple:

And at that time Solomon held a feast, and all Israel with him, a great congregation, from the entering in of Hamath unto the river of Egypt, before the LORD our God, seven days and seven days, even fourteen days.

(I Kings 8:65)

Other references are in Isaiah 30:29, Ezekiel 45:23, 45:25, Nehemiah 8:14 and II Chronicles 7:8.

The festival has both historical and national symbolism, as explained in Leviticus:

That your generations may know that I made the children of Israel to dwell in booths, when I brought them out of the land of Egypt: I am the LORD your God.

(Leviticus 23:43)

The universality of the festival is illustrated in the prophetic vision which sees all nations coming up to Jerusalem on the festival of Succoth, as declared by the prophet Zechariah:

And it shall come to pass, that every one that is left of all the nations which came against Jerusalem shall even go up from year to year to worship the King, the LORD of hosts, and to keep the feast of tabernacles.

(Zechariah 14:16; see also Isaiah 2:2–3, 56:6–8)

**Conclusion**

The acacia was the characteristic tree used by the Israelites in the wilderness, and symbolized the Ark of the Covenant and the Tabernacle, their center of ritual during their wanderings. When the people settled in the Land of Israel the Ark and the Tabernacle were placed in the Temple in Jerusalem. Zion symbolized the deep-rooted connection of the nation to its land and the people, who brought their choice fruits to the Temple on the Feast of Tabernacles. The preparations for this festival were much more prolonged than any other for the upland Israelite farmer, particularly in the Judean Hills. The vine growers would go out to the vineyards with their entire household to bring in the vintage, and this took the whole month of Elul. As related in Isaiah:

And the daughter of Zion is left as a cottage in a vineyard….

(Isaiah 1:8)

Succoth was the most important festival in the Jewish calendar, since it was celebrated in the autumn, the harvest time of all agricultural products. This is the season when the farmer assessed his successes and failures on the land over the year, while giving thanks to the Creator for the rain and dew that nourish the land, and praying for His blessing for the coming year. The Jewish Law states:

On the feast of Tabernacles, they are judged for water.

(*Rosh Hashana* 1:2)

And the Talmud declares:

The Holy One, Blessed be He, said, Pour out water before Me on Tabernacles, so that your rains this year may be blessed.

(*Rosh Hashana* 16a)

The four species taken for the festival ritual, the lulab (palm branch), the ethrog (citron), myrtle and willow, all require plentiful water supply for their growth.

In Isaiah 4:5–6 we find beautiful imagery relating to the two symbols that unite into one: the pillar of cloud by day and the fire by night and the *succah* in the wilderness, and the Temple and defence in Zion, both of which protect the people of Israel—the former in its youth during the period of wanderings in the wilderness, after the Giving of the Law, and the latter when the nation took root in its homeland:

And the LORD will create upon every dwelling place of mount Zion, and upon her assemblies, a cloud and smoke by day, and the shining of a flaming fire by night: for upon all the glory shall be a defence.

And there shall be a tabernacle for a shadow in the daytime from the heat, and for a place of refuge, and for a covert from storm and from rain.

(Isaiah 4:5–6)

The connection between the *succah* and Jerusalem is expressed in Psalms:

In Salem also is his tabernacle [*succah*], and his dwelling place in Zion.

(Psalms 76:2)